What the 1% KNOW

HOW EVERYDAY PEOPLE USE REAL ESTATE TO BUILD WEALTH

Robert Sayre

Internet addresses given in this book were accurate at the time it went to press.

Printed in the United States of America

Published in Hellertown, PA

Cover and interior design and illustrations by Christina Gaugler

ISBN 978-1-9524811-0-9

Library of Congress Control Number: 2021903970

2 4 6 8 10 9 7 5 3 1 paperback

Bright
COMMUNICATIONS   BrightCommunications.net

CONTENTS

INTRODUCTION
How to Use This Book

DO YOU WANT TO LEARN the real estate-investing, wealth-building secrets of the 1%?

In this book, you will find personal stories—my own as well as those of a few others who generously gave their time and insight. My story and the four case studies are accounts of my journey, including a few of my successes and failures. There are also interviews with other investors—all with unique, inspiring stories as well. Savor these. All of them have used investing in real estate to pursue their unique goals.

You will meet Maria Francesca Dattilo, who flips and builds houses. You will meet Anna, a woman who grew up poor in Section 8 housing, but, through grit and grace, built a six-figure income and then was able to replace that with income from her real estate investments, while supporting her husband's business and raising four children. You will meet Phil, a professional engineer who works at a large hospital, manages 25 rental units, and is raising his two young children with his wife. You will meet April, who gave birth to her son at age 16, went on to finish high school and college, and created a career in the health-care industry. At the age of 36, she retired from that job to devote herself to real estate investing. Two words that describe her are *honest* and *giving*. You will meet Steve, who began his career about 40 years ago, has built affordable housing, and has flipped and/or owned more than 1,000 units. You will meet Julia, a semi-retired wife and mother who, along with her husband, acquired three units that help them in their retirement. The equity on those buildings helped them purchase a business that her husband and son own and run.

I tried to go from the big ideas down to the very practical details. No book can cover all that is needed, and my own experience is unique, but certainly not comprehensive. The resources section includes books that have helped me as well as others learn.

I have found that real estate investment is lucrative and is truly a path to creating wealth. I wish I had started sooner. There is also something about restoring a property that is badly in need of repair. It becomes a home for a family—a place where memories can be made. That is inspiring.

The real estate-investment community is very generous. This may be surprising to people not in it, but if you encounter a problem, need advice, or can't find a plumber or someone who can deal with a leaky basement, you can find answers in this community—quickly and with a generous spirit. The community also gives back to other real estate investors, using money that they earned via their own blood, sweat, and tears.

There is great wisdom in this community—about investing and also about life. One thing I have found common among people who have succeeded in real estate is that they are continuous learners. They have all failed and gotten back up again and were smart and humble enough to look at their experiences and learn from them.

Another thing I've found to be common among real estate investors is that they work hard to accomplish their goals—though everyone featured in this book had different goals. Some were trying to leave their 9-to-5 jobs, others continue to work and invest on the side, and still others entered later in life, after retirement—like me. One of my challenges was to avoid comparing myself to others, pursuing the goals that made sense for me.

As you read the following pages, I hope you can glean some nuggets of wisdom that will lead you to pursue your own goals with gusto and meaning.

CHAPTER 1

My Story

MOST PEOPLE UNDERSTAND that buying and owning your own home is desirable. The concept that it is better to be buying something you will eventually own rather than "just paying rent" is readily understood. It used to be that there were very clear tax advantages to deduct the interest on your mortgage on your federal income taxes. But beyond that, real estate investing—in houses other than the one in which you live—seemed like the endeavor of the super wealthy. Investing in real estate seemed to be for people who had riches already to invest and had some "secret" knowledge or contact with people already in the industry. This was my view for most of my working career.

When I was growing up in the 1960s, my parents both worked as elementary school teachers to pay their mortgage on our modest home. My mother grew up on a homestead ranch in western Nebraska. A homestead ranch was land a person claimed under the Homestead Act of 1863. The Homestead Act was signed into law by President Abraham Lincoln the same year he wrote the Emancipation Proclamation. This allowed residents, mostly of Western states, to stake or file a claim for land owned by the federal government and receive a patent or title to the land if they improved the land. This included building some kind of shelter and other improvements on plots of land up to 160 acres.

My maternal grandfather was born in 1890 on a homestead ranch. My grandmother, having grown up on a ranch as well, was able to go to a "normal school," which at that time was something like a college for women, giving them some credentials. She became a teacher and began teaching in a one-room schoolhouse at the age of 18, in 1908. In the next seven years, she "proved up" (satisfied the government's requirements for obtaining land) and acquired 648 acres of ranchland while she taught children of other ranchers.

When my grandparents married in 1915, they combined their holdings to create a ranch of more than 1,300 acres. Over the years, they had proved up their own claims, and they also purchased land from others who wanted to get out or who gave up. When my grandparents sold that land and moved to Colorado, just prior to the Great Depression in 1929, they had some capital to start their new life.

On the ranch, my grandparents created income from their ranchland, raising cattle to sell. It was a hard life—one they left with few regrets. That income, like any other job, had to be replaced. My grandfather became a lifetime employee of what became Safeway, one of the largest supermarket companies at the time. He retired from there in 1955. Part of his compensation was stock in this public company. This was the basis of his retirement income on which he lived until he passed away in 1985 at 95 years of age.

Land and real estate created lasting assets that allowed my grandparents to build a life for their family where I grew up in Boulder. My grandfather was able to help my two siblings and four cousins attend college, a great aspiration for my grandfather, who had only an eighth-grade education.

My grandparents were able to create equity via the Homestead Act and by working and living on this land. This is very similar to the modern activity of house hacking, which is beginning investing with very little money by renting out part of your own house, or by acquiring a property with a rental included.

Growing up, we had Sunday dinner at my grandparents' house twice a month. Their modest two-bedroom home had an apartment in the basement they rented out to college students. They were always landowners and investors in one way or another.

My wife's parents were also involved in real estate, but from a different perspective. Her father, born in 1903, was a medical doctor who began practicing medicine prior to World War II. He also owned a series of small restaurants in Indianapolis that he ran while going through medical school in the 1920s. Her mother was born in 1915. Her parents wed after WWII.

After the marriage, my wife's mother never again worked outside the home. Instead, she took some of her husband's earnings, bought houses, and sold them "on contract." She acted like the bank and sold them with interest, amortized just like the banks did. She did this consistently over 30 years, making a good living, sometimes better than her husband. She acquired quite a few assets that allowed her to live independently until the age of 98, paying for all the home health care she required as she aged.

My wife and I knew this history, but we never put two and two together to consider investing in real estate ourselves. We were busy making a living, raising our kids, and trying to contribute to society in whatever ways we could. Sound familiar? Not until I was almost ready to retire did it start to click. My wife and I had always worked, and we had purchased a home and built equity in it simply by paying down the loan over decades. And of course, we ended up paying three times more due to being on the wrong side of compounding interest.

I was infused with the entrepreneurial spirit at an early age, which is helpful in real estate investing. When I was a junior in high school, my brother, who is six years older than me, had just returned from a two-year stint in Vietnam with the U.S. Marines. My mother, ever the industrious one, purchased a beekeeping business with the help of my grandfather: 125 hives, beekeeping equipment, a 1940 International pickup truck, and accounts in all of the budding health-food stores in the area and even in numerous grocery stores. I sure wish I had kept that truck! My mother's goal was to provide work for my brother. He had other plans, though, and soon was off to India in search of enlightenment. This left my mother and me to run the business. She was still a full-time teacher, so I ended up being the main worker.

I learned so much from Ted Johnson, my grandfather's friend from whom they purchased the business. I jumped headfirst into the unknown. Mr. Johnson was retiring at age 90 in late 1969, mostly because his wife was pressuring him to. He took me to every beeyard, opened up the hives with me, explained what he was doing, and had me follow him. This was his art—a lifetime of listening to "his bees"—and he seemed to enjoy imparting some of this to me.

Mr. Johnson took me to the grocery stores and introduced me to the managers so they knew who I was. He also taught me how to stock the shelves, to get paid, and to handle myself. My mother tagged along as much as she could and helped me do the work in the beeyards in the summers and also extract honey, bottle it, and label it for sale.

After three years, we sold the business. I wanted to move on, and the work was much more than my mother could handle. It was an incredible experience, and the notion of forging your own destiny was firmly implanted in me.

My wife and I began real estate investing when I was 62 and she was 65, one year from retiring from her work as a public school teacher. We had a basic retirement lined up, both with social security, her pension, my modest pension from a private company, and my 401k. We could live. But could we afford to have a great and exciting life? Perhaps not. Our adventures in real estate began a lot late. But as the Chinese proverb goes: The best time to plant a tree was 20 years ago. The second best time is now.

I thought I was a savvy businessman. I had held responsible financial positions in publishing companies—one with revenues of $260 million. I was the business manager, which sounded important. It was a great company and a good position. But in reality, my financial literacy was limited at best. What I did understand was that no one gets more than 24 hours in a day—not Bill Gates, not Steve Jobs, not Warren Buffett, and not you or me.

Can an old dog learn new tricks? The answer is yes, but it requires a willingness to read, invest in your own understanding, listen to others, and take calculated risks. This book is about that journey. We are not real estate moguls. Many people have had greater success and more experience. But our journey is ours. It has been a liberating and inspiring road to travel on. People will find our story to be relevant and the lessons applicable. With this book, I hope to create an asset to bring insight to you, spur you to action, and provide you with another source of income.

CHAPTER 2

The Big Picture

How do you measure wealth? Certainly, wealth as measured in terms of money is not the only standard, but for the purposes of this chapter, let us focus on that.

When I really started thinking about how people build wealth, I realized that the dividing line between people of means and those struggling is a simple fact: People of means have assets that make them money 24/7. They are the ones who have a higher level of wealth and well-being. This could be savings or investments in stocks and bonds. It could be unique patents or copyrighted material, such as songs or books. It could be a business, though many businesses are really just jobs.

Do not get me wrong: Jobs via businesses should be respected and valued. But many businesses are limited by the number of hours in a day.

The most accessible form of wealth creation is real estate. This has always been true... and still is. The simple logic of understanding that buying a home is better than renting one is true. It's still the dream of most families.

If you own a small business, ask yourself: Could it run independently of your daily management and leadership for a week? The answer is probably yes. How about a month? Many might be able to say yes. How about a year? Few business owners could answer yes to that. Does your business have a track record of positive cash flow in good times and bad? If your answer to the last two questions is yes, then your business could likely be considered an asset. Next ask: Would a bank or other financial institution lend you money based upon that cash flow and perceived viability? If the answer to that question is yes, your business is in a small pool of enterprises.

Would the value of your enterprise go up over time just because you continue to own and maintain it? If you are operating or considering running a small business, these are goals you should be aiming for. If you own a small business, have you considered buying the real estate it occupies?

How about owning other real estate? In chapter 3 and the interview with Anna Kelley (see page 26), you will learn about the unique aspects of real estate. I would like now to introduce some basic accounting concepts and their application, developed by entrepreneur and author Robert T. Kiyosaki.

Balance sheet: Your assets minus your liabilities, which equals your equity or the net of the two.

Asset: A resource with economic value that an individual, corporation, or country owns or controls with the expectation that it will provide a future benefit. Assets are reported on a company's balance sheet and are bought or created to increase a firm's value or benefit a firm's operations.

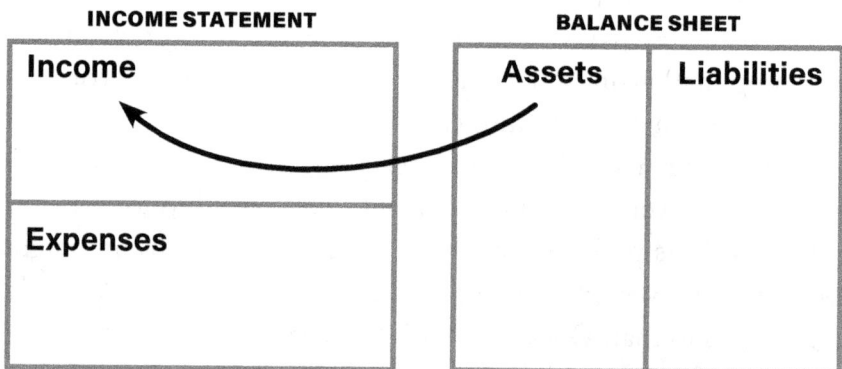

INCOME STATEMENT		BALANCE SHEET	
Income		Assets	Liabilities
Expenses			

An asset contributes to your income or cash flow.

Liability: Something a person or company owes, usually a sum of money. Liabilities are recorded on the right side of the balance sheet. They include loans, accounts payable, mortgages, deferred revenues, bonds, warranties, and accrued expenses.

Income statement: Your income minus your expenses. Pretty simple, right?

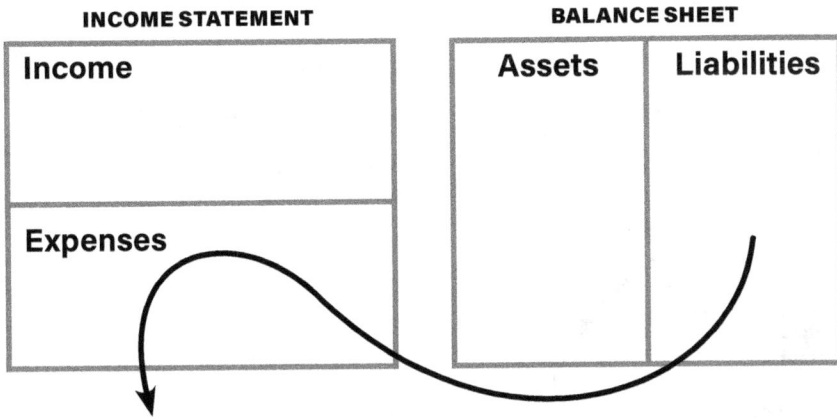

INCOME STATEMENT   BALANCE SHEET

Income		Assets	Liabilities
Expenses			

A liability is an expense or bill that is spent or withdrawn from your income.

You do not need to understand the nuts and bolts of accounting to understand these ideas.

Over the past two centuries, about 90 percent of the world's millionaires have been created by investing in real estate. For the average investor, real estate offers the best way to develop significant wealth.

How do you harness these concepts to your benefit? And how are these concepts reflected in daily life? Have you ever wondered how the cash flows of the poor, middle class, and wealthy really differ?

Cash Flow of the Poor

This image depicts the cash flow of people who live paycheck to paycheck, have little to no savings, and rent their place of residence. All of their income goes directly to pay expenses. Not all of the people in this category earn low wages. Some of them have fairly high incomes. Are you here? If yes, there is always time to act. The interviews in this book should inspire you. They come from people from all walks of life, not unlike you.

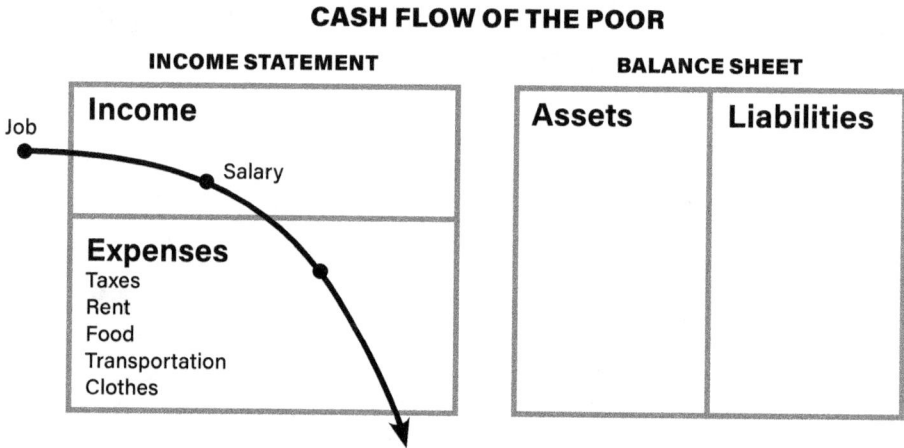

CASH FLOW OF THE POOR

INCOME STATEMENT	BALANCE SHEET

Job

Income

Salary

Expenses
Taxes
Rent
Food
Transportation
Clothes

Assets | **Liabilities**

Cash Flow of the Middle Class

How about the middle class? These are people who work for others. They might be making a lot of money, but they are still broke at the end of each month. A lot of people work very hard to attain this status. It is no small feat, and if this is where you are, you should be congratulated.

Middle class salaries are eroded by liabilities and then completely taken out by expenses. They are trading their time for dollars. If you're in this class, you're making ends meet, but you could be devastated financially if you lose your job or something happens that's completely out of your control. Are you saving enough money to someday stop working and retire?

CASH FLOW OF THE MIDDLE-CLASS

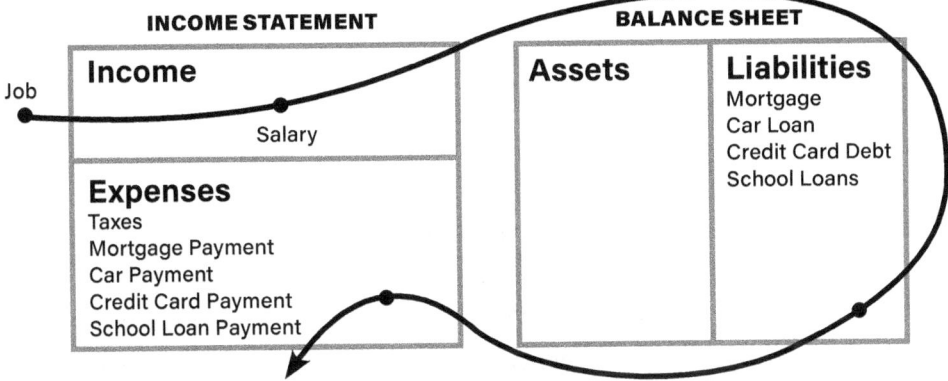

INCOME STATEMENT

BALANCE SHEET

Job

Income

Salary

Expenses
Taxes
Mortgage Payment
Car Payment
Credit Card Payment
School Loan Payment

Assets

Liabilities
Mortgage
Car Loan
Credit Card Debt
School Loans

Cash Flow of the Wealthy

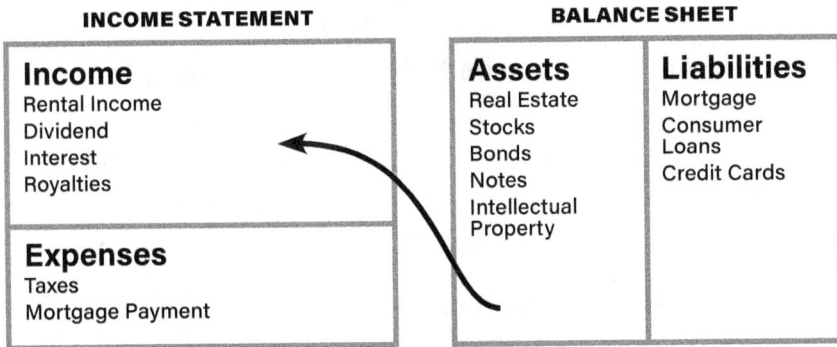

Herein lies the difference between the middle class and the poor and the wealthy. In addition to their salaries, the wealthy supplement income with assets, such as real estate. This allows them to have a surplus—more than enough to cover their liabilities and expenses. The wealthy own assets that pay them money 24/7.

CASH FLOW OF THE WEALTHY

INCOME STATEMENT

BALANCE SHEET

Income
Rental Income
Dividend
Interest
Royalties

Expenses
Taxes
Mortgage Payment

Assets
Real Estate
Stocks
Bonds
Notes
Intellectual
Property

Liabilities
Mortgage
Consumer
Loans
Credit Cards

Consider your cash flow, assets, and liabilities. If you are in the middle class, great job! If you want to go beyond this, to have monthly accounting procedures that allow you to pay your bills and a lot more, stay tuned. Investing in real estate is not beyond your grasp. It is the best source of income, stability, and long-term wealth creation. Read on to find out how.

These images have been inspired by illustrations in Rich Dad, Poor Dad *by Robert T. Kiyosaki.*

Maria Francesca Dattilo

Maria graduated from Immaculata University, with a major in psychology and a minor in education. She obtained a master's degree and pursued a career in counseling. She never thought she would wind up renovating, flipping, and even building houses, but now she is totally invested in it. She lives in Montgomery County, Pennsylvania, where she works with her husband and brother on their investment projects. She also works as a Realtor and is passionate about assisting her clients to buy, sell, and invest in real estate!

Robert: Was it always your goal to invest in real estate?
Maria: Not at all! I knew I wanted to help people, but it would be a long journey before real estate ever entered the picture. I majored in psychology at Immaculata University. My goal was to run my own psychology practice out of my home while raising my family. My dad convinced me to take education courses, so I majored in psychology and minored in education. I did an internship in brain injury rehabilitation, and that's also where I worked after graduation. I was comfortable there and successful.

Robert: Did you own a house?
Maria: Yes, in 2009, at age 29, I bought my own home. I was super excited. It felt like a big leap for a single woman. I started doing renovation projects, including ripping out old flooring and installing tile. I thought, *This is great! This is fun! I love it!* I discovered that I love using tools and learning how to fix things. I began watching HGTV nonstop—and thinking about flipping houses.

Robert: How did you learn about investing in real estate?
Maria: At first, I didn't know where to begin. I knew I wanted a broad base of knowledge before attempting to flip a house. Then, I realized I could take night classes in real estate while still working full-time.

Next, I started researching real estate companies. I found a list of the top 100 companies to work for. Keller Williams was number one on the list. There were two locations nearby, so I met with their recruiter. I took courses there for about three years.

I quickly learned I wasn't able to do real estate only part-time. But I was still so comfortable in my 9-to-5 job. It took me six years to find the courage to leave to do real estate full-time. *I gotta take a chance*, I realized. *I gotta jump in—both feet first. If it doesn't work, it doesn't work. There's always something else.*

Robert: And so you jumped?
Maria: Yes! I took a leap of faith, left my 9-to-5 job, and focused on real estate full-time: marketing, getting clients, and paying the bills.

Although my father initially expressed concern over me entering real estate, once he saw how passionate I was about it, he would later say, "If you can just keep your head above water until you make it, you'll be fine. In time, you'll get there." My brother was supportive of me from the very beginning though.

I threw myself into my new venture. I loved it all. When I was pregnant, I worked on a house, tiling a shower, until the day before I went into labor. I didn't want to just sit around waiting to go into labor. I remember thinking, *I have stuff to do. I have a house to flip!* My mom and husband tried to convince me to "take it easy and rest" but I wanted to work. I enjoy renovating.

Robert: So, did the real estate work lead to flipping houses?
Maria: Yes. As much as I enjoyed my new real estate job, renovating a home was always in the back of my mind. One of my clients wanted to sell her mother's house. She warned me that the house needed a lot of work. I thought, *This could be the house I've been looking for.*

When I saw the house, it was a disaster. But in my mind, it was an ice-cream sundae with a cherry on top. My brother and I bought it with the goal of fixing it up and flipping it. We hired an architect and home inspector and learned that the house needed even more work than we thought. Rather than renovating it, we simply relisted it, sold it, and made a profit.

Robert: And did you use that money to buy your next house to flip?
Maria: Yes. With that money, we bought a tiny three-bedroom Cape Cod. It was a perfect starter project. We fixed it up and sold it. Then, with that money, we bought a large 1900s Victorian, which needed several costly renovations. Eventually, we sold it and didn't lose any money.

A contractor I was working with recommended finding a lot and building new houses on it. We found not one but two lots side-by-side in Phoenixville, Pennsylvania. Friends and family invested money with us to buy the lots: my mom, brother, father-in-law, and a Realtor friend.

Each step looked very challenging—more like mountains really. But as we moved along, they looked simpler, probably because of working through more and more challenges. Soon, they didn't feel like challenges anymore, just the next steps in the journey.

Robert: Were you nervous investing other people's money?
Maria: I kept asking myself how we would raise the money. But friends and family were actually eager to invest. It felt like the money just appeared. It was incredible. I wasn't nervous, not even afraid really. I asked my friends, "What do I have to be afraid of? This is a calculated risk. Homes have value."

I believed deeply that this was going to work. I told myself, *This is what I'm going to do,* and then I just did it. Telling you now, it sounds so crazy, but I think that's what following your dreams should be.

Looking back, it feels like this was all meant to happen in my life—in this way and at this time. For 14 years, I helped people in the health-care field, but my interest in real estate and flipping houses was always there in the back of my mind. I knew I would regret it if I didn't try. At one point, I was dreading regret more than I was worried about taking on a new venture. That's when you know you have to take a risk. That's when it's time to jump.

When you tell yourself it's what you're going to do and you stick to it, you're committed to that idea. You're dedicated to it. You seek out what you need, and the answers just come. You look for the people, and they present themselves. You ask for the money, and you get it. You put it out to the universe, and then you just find a way to make it happen. Each step just presents itself.

After we built the twin houses, we found another lot, engineered it, and were approved to build four houses in the next year.

Robert: What are your future plans?

Maria: I want to continue to renovate and flip houses as well as find land and build homes. I'd like to take on even bigger projects, such as renovating a warehouse or church into apartments, and I'd also like to do custom features to a client's liking. I can't imagine what the future will hold, but I do see us reaching the point where my brother and I earn a full salary from our business, and enough passive income to retire at 50 if we choose to! I'm going to keep moving forward.

You can't give in to the fear of taking the risk. In fact, maybe give in to the fear of regret. You don't want to regret not taking the risk later. When the fear of regret is greater than the fear of the risk, that's when you know you have to take a chance. You're ready.

Maria Francesca Dattilo
Golden Lion Tamarin, LLC
484-614-8074
Dattilo1015@gmail.com

CHAPTER 3

The Unique Aspects of Real Estate Investing

REAL ESTATE INVESTING is different from other types of investing. Learning about the unique aspects of real estate so that you can feel confident in making decisions using these concepts, and harnessing them to benefit yourself and your family, is probably the most important lesson in this book. The case studies and insights from interviews with other investors will highlight how they can be applied to your life and journey toward financial independence. Here are some key real estate investing terms you'll need to understand to begin investing.

Cash Flow

After you've collected your rent and paid your expenses, such as your mortgage, property taxes, insurance, maintenance, and property management company, the money you have left over is your cash flow. If you are receiving more money in rent than you're paying in expenses, your cash flow is positive. That's, of course, the goal! If you are paying more in expenses than you're receiving in rent, your cash flow is negative. Time to make a change! One of the main reasons people fail in business is that they don't understand cash flow.

Appreciation

Appreciation is the rising of home prices over time. Home prices fluctuate—going up and also down—but in the long run, over time, real estate values have always gone up. That's how the majority of wealth is built in real estate. When people make a really significant amount of money in real estate, it's due to appreciation.

Appreciation is a long-term benefit. While it's quite reliable over the long term, it alone should not be the primary reason to acquire a property. In any time period and market, the value of a property can decline, and the factors contributing to this are largely beyond your control.

Depreciation

Despite what the word implies, depreciation is not the value of real estate dropping. It is actually a tax term describing your ability to write off part of the value of the asset itself every year. This significantly reduces the tax burden on the money you make, providing one more reason why real estate protects your wealth while also growing it.

Each year, if you own residential real estate, you can write off 1/27.5 of the property's value (the value of the building, not the land) against the income you've generated. For example, if you bought a house for $200,000, you would divide that number by 27.5 to get $7,272. This is the amount you could write off the cash flow you earned for the year from that property. Many times, this is more than the entire cash flow, and you can avoid taxes completely.

Other Deductible Business Expenses

Depreciation is not the only item that can reduce your taxable income. Related business expenses such as traveling can also. You should always consult with a qualified CPA to determine which business expenses can legally reduce your taxable income, but for now, be aware that there are many.

Taxes

Income from real estate is taxed differently than income from work. First, when you receive income from a job or any activity that produces a W-2, taxes are deducted from your gross income, such as Social Security, Medicare, and federal, state, and local income taxes. With real estate income, you are able to deduct expenses such as depreciation and business expenses such as insurance, property taxes, and other items first before calculating your taxable income. Second, real estate income is taxed at different rates than earned income—most of the time at lower rates. This is a little-understood benefit to real estate investing, and it is available to the investor at any level. Be sure to discuss this with your CPA or tax adviser.

Leverage

Leverage is an investment strategy of using borrowed money to increase the potential return of an investment. When you borrow money for a real estate investment, you pay it back on a predetermined payment schedule just like any other loan. Real estate is one of the easiest assets to leverage—maybe the easiest. Banks and lenders feel comfortable valuing what property is worth so you can leverage money against that property. By putting a small amount of money down, you're able to get a mortgage. For example, interest rates are currently below 5%, down payments can be 20% or less, and loans are routinely amortized over 30-year periods. What else can you invest in using financing with terms like that?

Many business enterprises are more or less a way to create a job. This is a time-honored tradition, and in the words of my grandfather, "All work is valuable." But few businesses would be considered assets by a bank or lender. Real estate is! Being able to leverage these assets gives you an amazingly effective tool.

Loan Pay Down

A pay down applies to any type of loan; you are simply making regular payments to pay off the debt. When you have a car loan, student loan, or mortgage, you are making the payments toward your debt. When you take out a loan to invest in real estate, however, you typically pay it back with the rent money from the tenants. You have cash flow, and you are also slowly paying down your loan balance with each payment to the bank. Just like when you pay your own mortgage, the principal is paid down over time and the equity is built up. With a rental property, the tenant is making those payments and you, as the owner, reap the benefits.

Forced Equity

Forced equity is a powerful term in real estate. It's the equity you instantly put into a property when you make improvements to it. By improving a home, you increase the home's market value, and you also increase the market rent, which means you can make more money each month and pay off your property faster.

Unlike appreciation, where you are at the mercy of the market and factors you can not control, forced equity gives you control. It gives you an option to have a hand in increasing your property's value.

The most common example of forced equity is buying a fixer-upper property and improving its condition. If you can pay below market value for a property that needs upgrades, then add appliances, new flooring, and paint, it's a great way to create wealth through real estate without much risk.

While this is the most common method, it's not the only one. Another way to force equity is to fix up the property when a tenant moves out, which allows you to then rent it for more money to the next tenant. Another idea is if you have a multiple-unit rental, maybe you could add a laundry facility, for which you'll earn income from the use of the washers and dryers. Or, maybe you can convert to a more-efficient, less-expensive heating system to reduce your heating costs.

Inflation

Inflation is the decline of purchasing power of a given currency over time. But how does inflation affect real estate prices? In general, our money supply overall is worth less and less with each passing year. As the value of money decreases, the price of goods and services increases. For example, if you put $20,000 under your mattress for 10 years, what that money could purchase would be much less due to inflation. Many of us take this for granted and don't think about it much. We accept that prices go up. While it's easy to take for granted, inflation is actually an incredibly powerful wealth-building tool when harnessed appropriately.

The reason why inflation helps build wealth in real estate is that the majority of big expenses (mortgage, property taxes) stay fixed for the majority of the time you own the property. When you combine this with rising rents and home values (which are also due to inflation), you start to see big results. If you know that it's reasonable to expect inflation to continue, why not invest in an asset where this will benefit you?

Anna Kelley

Anna Kelley grew up in San Antonio, Texas, in Section 8 housing. After college, she worked hard to build a career as a financial relationship manager to high-income investors at Bank of America and then AIG. Anna's story is one of persistence, grit, and grace. She lives with her husband and four children near Hershey, Pennsylvania. She is currently working with other investors to put together large syndication deals.

Robert: What is the real estate acronym IDEAL?
Anna: In real estate, IDEAL implies that real estate is an ideal investment compared to all the other investment alternatives out there in the retail world, such as stocks, bonds, mutual funds, and annuities.

- I is for income. Real estate investing generates an income, ideally, if you're buying right.

- D is for depreciation, which is paper losses that save you money on your taxes even though you're really making money. That's always a really good thing.

- E is for equity. This is where tenants pay off your mortgage in rental properties. That's how your net worth really grows. As properties go up in value, you create equity, which is more value than what you have in a mortgage. That's where real wealth comes in.

- A is for appreciation, which is the fact that very rarely does property actually go down in value. If you're maintaining a property, it's usually going to go up in value and create more wealth over time.

- L is for leverage. With most institutional retail investments, you can't get a loan to invest. For example, you can't borrow money to invest in the stock market. With real estate, you can borrow money. The power of leverage is being able to borrow 80% of the value of that investment; you only have to put 20% into it. That's what makes the average American able to invest in real estate.

Robert: To leverage with stocks and bonds means that you have to take gigantic risks. People do it. I'm sure people do make money in that, but it's extremely risky and complex, right?

Anna: Right. And you're borrowing on speculation. Usually, stock market leverage is only available to people who already have a lot of money (unless you're just going to borrow from a credit card to invest in the stock). You have no control over that stock or its value.

With real estate, you borrow money with a reasonable certainty of how to control that investment to make sure you can cover that mortgage payment. It's much less risky if you're investing in the right kind of properties.

When I graduated from college, I worked in the private bank department at Bank of America, handling the wealth of the bank's top 10% customers. We showed them how they could grow their wealth by using our products, including annuities, insurance products, stocks, bonds, and mutual funds. I knew a lot about traditional retail investments, and I could tell people how to grow their wealth and meet their financial goals. But I didn't know anything about real estate.

At the time, I didn't have any of my own money to invest. I started wondering how I could build real wealth—even though I had little money to start with.

I started thinking about investing in real estate. I didn't

want to waste money on renting an apartment, so I bought a small condo that I started to rent out. My husband and I also owned another rental property in Houston.

In 2007, my husband and I moved to central Pennsylvania so he could start his own business in his hometown. We looked for a location to lease. At that time, leasing space was very, very expensive. Instead, I found a building to buy. It was in a perfect location, but it came with three tenants and four garages.

At first, my husband and I were reluctant to become landlords. But we realized that the income generated by the rental units would cover the mortgage on the property—with money to spare.

We thought the income would make any headaches from the tenants worth it. It would actually be much less risky to own the property and rent most of it out, than it would have been to lease space for a new business. I suddenly understood the power of real estate income.

Real estate investing was so new to me that I didn't know anything about leverage, appreciation, or depreciation. That rental property was so successful for my husband and I that we decided to house hack another building; we would live in part of the building and rent out the rest. We were able to borrow 97% of the value of the property.

Our family lived in one unit, and we rented out the other three units. It was really a protectionary move, covering our mortgage by the rental income. I knew that if I lost my job and my husband's new business didn't go well, at least we would have rental income to buy food and cover our mortgage.

We left our big home in Houston, and squished with our 3-year-old and 10-month-old children into a tiny apartment. It felt like a big step back at the time. But my husband and I knew that the sacrifice would be worth it to build his business and work toward my goal of staying home with our kids.

Then, the economy collapsed.

In 2009, I was employed by AIG, working with ultra-high-net-worth investors. AIG was in the news every day—and not in a good way. I feared losing my job. My husband's business was just getting started, and it was burdened with more than $700,000 in start-up debt.

We're going to have no income, I worried. *We've got to do something.*

Then things got worse. Within a few weeks, I lost about two-thirds of the money in my 401k, which we're taught as financial advisers can never happen. Well, it did. All I had left to my name was the remaining one-third of my 401k. So, I did what financial advisers always advise against: I borrowed from it.

I found another four-unit building for sale. I calculated that I could borrow the 20% down payment from my 401k, get a mortgage for the remaining 80%, and pay myself back with interest. Suddenly, I realized I could leverage my 401k and a bank loan to buy a property that would then earn me $1,200 to $1,600 a month. Now I understood the power of leverage!

I thought, *I may lose my job. My husband may lose his business. But we will make it.*

Then I found out I was pregnant.

Well, we will be really poor, but at least we can eat, I thought.

As the rental payments came each month, I learned that the rental properties were more valuable and stable than any job or entrepreneurial productivity. Even during the recession, our tenants paid rent. As the value of the property went up, I understood the power of appreciation.

I quickly learned that rental properties appreciate in a different way from single-family homes you live in. Your home appreciates by "natural appreciation." Its value generally appreciates, or grows in value over time, which usually is around 3% a year.

But with multi-family rental properties, you can force the appreciation, making it go up faster. The value of a multi-family property is highly reliant on the net operating income that you can produce. The more you can raise rents and cut expenses, the more the net operating income increases. Therefore, the value of the property goes up equivalent to how much you've been able to increase that income.

My husband and I quickly realized that if we fixed the units up, we could raise the rents by $200 or $300 more per month. We put all of our time and energy into fixing up the units. We increased the value, and then we raised the rents. At the same time, we also cut our expenses. There are many ways to do that, for example, you could have the tenants take on some maintenance or you could reduce your insurance. We forced the appreciation quickly, by making improvements, reducing costs, and raising rents to reflect that value we created significant equity in that building.

How? We borrowed when the property was valued at one price, and then we improved it to make it worth a lot more. This created equity in the property. We took second mortgages on the properties that we had for the difference in that equity. By doing this, we created more value and equity. We refinanced and took that equity to use as the down payment on the next one, and the next one, and the next one. This is called the Buy, Repair, Rent, Refinance, Repeat method (BRRRR). We were succeeding, and I still didn't understand the power of depreciation!

Robert: Depreciation can be difficult to understand—until you get your tax bills and realize, "Oh, my goodness!"

Anna: After a few months of owning the multi-family rental property, I started to learn about depreciation from my accountant. Depreciation is a great tax benefit to real estate investing. Even though you make money every month on your property, you get to show that you have a loss against it. This makes your net income very low. In the beginning, your net income might even be negative.

For an easy example, if I buy a property worth $275,000, I can deduct $10,000 each year as depreciation losses against my income, decreasing my taxes. Depreciation gives a huge incentive to buy property and not have to pay taxes on the income for quite some time.

Before people understand depreciation, they only consider their cash-on-cash return. They think, I put $10,000 down on a building. It's going to give me $10,000 a year in net income from rent. That's a 100% return on my money.

But it's even better than that. That income is just one piece of your total return. To figure out your total return on a $10,000 investment, remember that your mortgage is being paid down every single month, the tax deductions save you money that you would have paid in taxes, and because of appreciation, you will be able to sell the property later for more than you paid for it. Combined, this adds up to a really powerful return.

On the other hand, when you invest in stocks, all you have is maybe some distributions. You hope you have growth, but you're paying big taxes on that growth. You're also paying a lot of fees to own stocks. Your after-tax return from stocks is insignificant.

But when you buy property, your return on that 20% you put down can be significantly more than the average 8% return in the stock market. The returns on almost all of my properties are between 35% and 50%. But really, the returns are infinite because I'm able to pull out my equity. After I pull out my equity, I don't have anything invested anymore, and then it's just nothing but profits. Real estate investing is powerful, powerful, powerful. Truly the ideal investment is to buy small, multi-family rental properties.

Longing to stay at home with my kids, I created a five-year-plan to exit my job. I calculated that I could replace my six-figure income if I bought 12 units per year over the next five years, growing my portfolio to 60 units. I'd even have some extra for vacations!

Having lived through the collapse of 2009, I knew that I needed to learn about economic and real estate cycles. I needed to understand the causes of recessions and be able to identify the signs of a looming recession. I wasn't going to be blindsided again. I now had real estate investing income, but I also had incurred some debt from all the remodels. I knew the only way I would feel super safe leaving my job was if I sold a few buildings to pay down that debt. I earned a significant commission by putting together a big multi-family deal. I knew I needed to be wise and conservative. That's what gave me the confidence to leave my corporate job forever and enjoy the financial freedom that we've developed through our rental income.

I realized that I could create a group of investors to buy a big, multi-family property. As the deal maker and property finder, they would pay me a 3% acquisition fee. If I found a property worth $6 million, I'd earn a six-figure acquisition fee.

So, I started looking for a bigger multi-family deal. In a couple weeks, I found an off-market deal of a $6 million to $7 million property. I lined up my investor-partners to partner with me. I created that deal, got it done, and earned my acquisition fee.

Then I decided to refinance my house, pull out the equity, and keep investing. And then I retired. I had confidence to do that big deal because I had done it so many times before—just on a smaller scale. The big deal was just more units in one deal. I knew I needed to start branching out, working with others, partnering with others, to continue to grow and to feel safe that the wealth that I created and the income I created over those many years of investing really was going to last my entire lifetime, and that I would never need to go back to a corporate job again.

Robert: That's a great story. You did it!
Anna: I have worked with the wealthiest, most famous people and owners of big businesses. I've worked with their advisors to create really complicated hedge fund investments. I've worked with stocks, bonds, mutual funds, and alternative fuel investments. I am here to tell you that there is nothing like real estate. Nothing else can take you from a negative $700,000 net worth and make you a multimillionaire with a high six-figure income—in just a few years. Real estate is the IDEAL investment. If you put in the time and do the work, you can create wealth and achieve financial freedom that will last your lifetime—and, hopefully, the lifetime of your children as well.

Robert: What are your hopes for the future?
Anna: I grew up in Section 8 housing. I can be content in an apartment. Contentment is what you make of it, right? For me, contentment is having the power to live my life by design and do what I want to do with my time. I cherish my role as

a stay-at-home mom. But now that my kids are in school, I get to decide how to spend their school hours each day.

Financially, I don't have to work another day in my life. But would that bring me contentment? Would it be fulfilling to sit and think about myself all day? No, I want to give back. I want to do greater things.

My goal is to help other people. I've always been a person who tries to help other people. I've worked with underprivileged youth. I've worked with inner-city kids, and I really have a desire to help anyone really. I especially have a heart for single moms, working moms, and young people who don't have anyone to guide them and show them what's possible.

I've been through it. I want to help people see the power of what's available to them, to fast-track for them what took me years to learn—help them to get that first rental property under contract, teach them the IDEAL investment concept, and help them figure out how to invest in their first property. Nothing is more exciting to me than to see how that can change their lives.

It's so rewarding. I'm excited to see people take the steps to invest in their lives. They will change the financial trajectory of their entire lives.

Anna Kelley
GreaterPurposeCapital.com
GreaterPurposeCapital.com
anna@greaterpurposecapital.com
Facebook: Anna Reimom Kelley

Buy, Repair, Rent, Refinance, Repeat

It was 2016, and with the advice of a friend and colleague who advised us to learn one thing well first, before trying other types of investments, my wife and I were looking for our first *real* real estate investment. This was not our first investment, but it was the first we had sourced, funded, and put on the market ourselves. My wife and I agreed that we would invest some of our retirement funds to purchase a rental property.

I had met people who were flipping properties (buying, repairing, and then selling), buying multi-units, and even purchasing apartment buildings. I needed a simpler goal to focus on, so we began to look at single-family row houses.

I looked for houses to buy in Reading, Allentown, Bethlehem, and Easton, Pennsylvania—communities within an hour of our home. I used Realtors as buyer's agents in each area who set up listings, some on the Multiple Listing Service (MLS), for me to walk through. Often the best deals aren't on the MLS. They're off-market properties—such as bank-owned properties, foreclosures, or estate sales—that need to be sold quickly and easily. I dedicated two days per week for house tours, and I told the Realtors to set up five or six houses to look at in their areas per day.

I discovered pretty quickly that the houses in Reading were in quite bad repair, and I don't know many contractors there I could hire to fix them up. The properties I saw in Bethlehem were too expensive for my calculations and sense of risk. After three months of searching and walking through about 50 houses, I found a property with the help of my Realtor in Allentown.

I have learned that not all Realtors are equal. Ones who are experienced in investment properties, or even better who are investors themselves, are extremely valuable. They are in touch with their market area and have vast experience and knowledge on the value of a property and how to consider your offer and negotiations. My Realtor, Carol, was invaluable in helping me find and negotiate this deal. Her 3% commission was money well spent. It is essential that you build trust in the industry as you build your team. Remember that your buyer's agent will also be representing you if you flip the house. If you plan to flip or sell the house, it's important to build your reputation as a trustworthy person to do business with.

Another important person on your team is your investment partner and/or spouse. Make sure your partner is on board with the broad parameters of what you are doing. This is critical for your relationship, and your partner can serve as a good sounding board. They do not need to be invested in learning or knowing as much as you, but being included in the broad parameters of your activity is crucial. In many cases, you are investing the equity in your home, your retirement funds, or at least your time. Your partner needs to understand your goals, enough details to make them comfortable, and the downside risks as well as the potential upsides.

The Allentown property we hoped to buy was owned by an investor couple. They were asking $54,000. I offered $43,500. I had noticed that their asking price had dropped $15,000 in $5,000 increments over five months. I knew that they were motivated sellers. They countered at $50,000, and I just waited. After six weeks, they came back and accepted my offer, if we could close within two weeks. I'll never know why they changed their minds, but I think they ran out of time for what they wanted to use that money for. I had been content to walk away from that deal, but in the back of my mind, I hoped we could buy it. This is a good lesson for anyone: Don't fall in love with any investment deal or house. You need to let the numbers determine the outcome and always keep active. Keep looking.

So, how did I determine my offer of $43,500? First, you need to determine the market value, or After Repair Value (ARV), of the property. To do this, you need to find another property that is as close as possible to an exact comparison of your property. Since my property was in a dense city area, my comparison property needed to be within a half-mile. It should also have sold within the past six months, but preferably three to four months. This meant that I was looking for row houses with 1,200 square feet, three bedrooms, and one bathroom. There were quite a few higher and some lower, but I came up with an ARV of $67,000, which my Realtor confirmed was reasonable. Next, I took 75% of that number, to get $50,500 (rounded up slightly). This number represents what a bank would likely refinance my property for.

Next, I subtracted the estimated costs of repairs necessary to make this house ready to rent, which in this case was quite low at only $2,000.

If you are unfamiliar with estimating costs pay a reliable construction professional to give you an estimate, which will cost only $100 to $200. It pays for their time if you choose not to go forward with a project, and you will also learn in the process. The house was in very good shape. This brought my maximum offer to $48,500. Finally, I deducted 10%, or about $5,000, as my negotiating margin to come to $43,500 as my initial offer. As it turned out, the seller finally accepted my offer of $43,500.

After Repair Value (ARV) Purchase Analysis

After Repair Value (ARV)	$67,000
Less bank refinance (75%)	$50,500
Less repairs to rent	$ 2,000
Maximum acceptable purchase price	$48,500
Less 10% negotiating margin	$5,000
Starting offer	$43,500

To get this house rent ready required only $2,000 of basic and cosmetic upgrades, so we have $45,500 all in. The cash flow looked promising.

At this point, it's important to crunch the numbers to make sure you can charge a high enough monthly rent to cover your costs and allow for profit. To do that, research the cost of comparable rents in your area. In our case, rents of three-bedroom, one-bathroom homes were around $900 to $1,000. I started with $925.

First, deduct 10% for property management. A property manager provides key services for the investor, though you may choose to self-manage. Typically, they charge one month's rent to find a tenant and 10% of the monthly rent to collect rent and handle all tenant communications, including finding handymen and other contractors to fix and repair the property, as needed.

Then, deduct your monthly insurance cost, in my case, $55 per month. Next, deduct your monthly taxes, here $185. After that, calculate a 10% allowance for vacancy and another 10% for repairs. This should be set aside or saved for the time those funds will be necessary. After these calculations, my total monthly costs were $517.50, leaving me with $407.50, a 44% profit.

Cash Flow for Rental Analysis

Square feet	1,264
Monthly rent	$925.00
Property management (10%)	$92.50
Insurance	$55.00
Taxes	$185.00
Vacancy allowance (10%)	$92.50
Repairs allowance (10%)	$92.50
Total costs	$517.50
Net profit (44%)	$407.50

To earn all my money back from this deal, I would have to keep it for 112 months, or about 9.3 years ($45,500/$407.50).

During our tenant's first year, I read several books about the concept of buy, repair, rent, refinance, and repeat. I talked with other investors at local meetups. I approached several banks and went through with refinancing this property after a year of owning it. Some banks require a specific period of time owning a property before you can refinance, but others do not. Check with local banks in your area.

The bank required an appraisal, which I paid for. The appraiser valued the property at $60,000. The bank would lend me 75% of the value of the property, $45,000. There were approximately $4,000 in costs for this transaction, so I came away with $41,000, and the new calculation for this property had changed.

After the refinance, we also raised the rent to $975.00 to reflect current market value.

Cash Flow after Refinancing

Square feet	1,264
Monthly rent	$975.00
Property management (10%)	$97.50
Insurance	$55.00
Taxes	$185.00
Mortgage	$332.00
Vacancy allowance (10%)	$97.50
Repairs allowance (10%)	$97.50
Total costs	$864.50
Net profit (11%)	$110.50

Because of the cash-out refinance and taking $41,000 out of the property, I now only had $4,000 invested, so the payback was only 36 months, or 3 years. And the best part in all this was I was able to pay off other debts with the $41,000, which saved me $1,300 per month! My wife had been supportive, but with these results, she was sold, all in. This one deal transformed our retirement!

Refinance Analysis

Bank determined value	$60,000
Less refinance (75%)	$45,000
Refinance costs	$4,000
Cash-out amount	$41,000
Mortgage	$332/month

We sold the property after 18 months, when the tenant left, for $78,564. After paying off the mortgage, we walked away with $29,000. We used most of this money to invest in another property, the other side of a duplex we lived in, so we could control that property and the tenants who lived next to us.

Sale Cash-Out Analysis

Sale price	$78,564
Sales commission (6%)	$4,714
Transfer tax (1%*)	$785
Other expenses	$1,534
Mortgage payoff	$42,515
Net profit**	$29,016

*This applies for my area of Pennsylvania. Check for your own area.
**There are capital gains taxes due on this; talk to your tax advisor.

This case study is a good example of several of the IDEAL concepts: income, depreciation, equity, appreciation, and leverage. This property provided income; the appreciation or increase in value allowed me to use the leverage in the value of the property to refinance it and get nearly all my investment out of it. We chose to pay off other debts as we were semi-retired. The appreciation in the value of the property in the market allowed us to sell it at a handsome profit and invest in a property that enhanced the value of our own home and increased the value of both.

Many investors use this BRRRR (Buy, Repair, Rent, Refinance, Repeat) method to build up their portfolio of properties, essentially recycling their one investment multiple times. Could you do this? Of course you could, but this does not happen without investing time to read, attend meetings, network with others, and put in the legwork to look at properties and build up your "team" to assist you.

Lessons Learned

- Perform due diligence in determining your ARV, with a real estate agent or on your own.
- Buy based upon cash flow, not appreciation. Appreciation is dessert.
- Learn to take calculated risks. You learn by doing.

CHAPTER 4

Getting Started

AFTER I STARTED INVESTING IN REAL ESTATE, more than one person had inquired about investing. One commented, "It seems like you have to keep a lot of balls in the air at one time." That is not untrue, but real estate is not really a complicated business. But it does require hard work, diligence, and grit at times.

Another interested party visited a house I had just bought. She said, "I would never live there. I hate the paneling, and the colors are just awful." The property manager who opened it up for us simply said, "I have never had a single potential renter turn down a property for those reasons, never!" This woman loaned me money at a handsome rate, which I used to secure another property, just like any other lien or mortgage, and it was paid off within six months. This is the value of private money lending, which is money borrowed from people, not banks. Many people are interested in real estate investing, but they might not want to do the work, or they might be too risk averse. They will lend money to people who are doing the actual investing.

Another person considering real estate investing, after looking at several potential deals, felt too nervous. It felt too risky for him. My advice was, "If you can't sleep well after you make a decision to invest, you should probably not pursue this."

You may be thinking, *I don't have enough money to do this. Don't you need to have a lot of money to invest?* You might be surprised to find out that money is not the biggest hurdle. Now, some people will try to tempt you into believing that you can do this with no money. While it's true that some have done it, this is not the norm. To do that, you have to really take risks, work harder than you probably ever have, and suffer more than one setback.

So just how does one start? As outlined in chapter 3, real estate is a unique asset. So, as an investor, the development of knowledge is *your* most important asset. Investing in yourself by taking the time to learn about keeping "all those balls in the air" gives you the confidence to make decisions and to take calculated risks. People who invest in real estate are as varied as any group: young and old, men and women, formally educated and some who never finished high school.

What skills do you need? If you can add, subtract, multiply, divide, and calculate percentages, you know enough math. Seriously, the math is not hard. There are aspects of investing that you can and likely should outsource to others. For example, let the CPAs do the tax returns. When you need an attorney, hire one. You can't replicate their training. You can learn the basics of how a house is put together, but you do not need to be a licensed plumber, electrician, or contractor. You need to be able to manage teams of people, provide clear direction, and follow up on their work. I will delve into more of the key skills in chapter 5.

Investing in yourself means reading, listening, and networking. Take a look at the resources and references in the back of this book. These are just a few; develop a daily habit of reading on the subject. Or listening: There are lots of really great podcasts. Tune in. And meet people. Attend meetups, connect with others, listen, ask questions, and make connections. I have found the real estate investing community to be very helpful, offering advice and insight easily and with a generous attitude toward you. Everyone had to start out somewhere, and I guarantee you that they were given a leg up by someone. Without exception, this is true. Find meetups and other business-oriented networking meetings, and attend them on a regular basis. Expect to do this for at least a year. In reality, one of the most common traits investors have is that they are lifelong learners. They may learn differently, but they are always seeking more information and acquired wisdom.

An attitude that you need to have is that mistakes and failure are opportunities for you to learn. If you have not done this yet, you will here. There are many strategies for making calculated decisions, and to have your mistakes be calculated, but you will make some. These are investments in yourself, an opportunity to learn and grow. I have also found that once people set off on the adventure of investing in real estate, they experience a quantum leap in their own personal development. Notice that I haven't talked about money so much? And yet, real estate is the clearest and most reliable path to wealth and financial independence.

One important lesson I learned is to never compare yourself—your goals, in particular—with others. There is a certain amount of bragging in this industry, which is a numbers game at times. How many doors do you have? How many do you plan to add in the next year? The next three to five years? I began at a much later time in my life than many others, so I was and still am not looking to create a huge empire or deal with the risk that it would involve. Take time to be comfortable with your initial goals, and work to achieve them. If they turn out to be too easy, you can always adjust them.

Another challenge is in building your team. This is covered in chapter 6, but when you start, it is okay to just put one foot in front of the other and learn as you go. Keep your promises; your word is critical in this industry. A good way to learn about contracting is to pay a contractor to view properties with you. Getting their opinion, even a rough idea, is valuable, and you can build a relationship from there. Respecting their time is very important.

The same is true with Realtors. They have great market insight, but they are paid only on commission, so I found that it's best to come really prepared and to be clear about the types of properties you are looking for, the area, and the price range. If you respect their time and ultimately close a deal with them, they will trust and want to work with you.

And what about all those courses, gurus, and mentors? Is this just a waste of money? Do they count as investing in myself as an asset? My experience is that they could, but there are some considerations. First, are you really willing to follow through on the advice given to you? If you are not ready to act, make decisions and need time to get a better sense of the market and what is involved, my advice is to wait. If you don't have the money, do what is necessary to cut some unnecessary expenses, find a way make it, or get it somehow. And make sure you do your own due diligence on the person and program. Does it mesh with how you learn, how you envision acting and arriving at a financial destination and position in three to five years? Make sure that you talk to people who have actually used the mentor or program before. When I worked in publishing, the editorial staff often said, "Everyone needs an editor." Even famous and gifted writers need editors. The same can be true with any profession or new pursuit.

I remember a story from Mike Krzyzewski, the famous basketball coach of the Duke University men's basketball team, who has led the Blue Devils to five NCAA Division I titles, 12 Final Fours, 15 ACC Men's Basketball Tournament championships, and 12 ACC regular season titles. He has also coached three Olympic teams that won gold medals. One of these teams included Michael Jordan, arguably the greatest basketball player of all time. What could this coach have to teach Michael Jordan? Certainly not how to shoot a jump shot or any of the basics of basketball. What he did provide was insight to the teams they were playing, what he or any other player could not see on the court. He could see patterns Jordan could not. So, did Michael Jordan need a coach? You bet. Does that mean you need to enroll in an expensive program or pay a coach or mentor? I think you will know when the time is right and the person or program is right.

Almost everyone I've met in real estate has used a coach or mentor, paid or not, at some point in the life of their business. This could be right out of the gate, or when you have enough experience to know what you don't know and what you do. You will need a coach or mentor when you need or want to reach a new level—when the territory and experience and information you need to make calculated risks is greater than where you are. Use this with discretion as you would with a lawyer, plumber, or electrician.

Phil Chadbourn

Phil came to Pennsylvania to attend Lehigh University, where he studied Industrial Engineering. He was also trained in Lean Six Sigma process improvement strategies. He currently works at a large health system and lives in Bethlehem, with his wife and two children, while managing a 25-unit investment portfolio.

Robert: When did you get started in investing?

Phil: After college I had a roommate who was "born" into real estate, and he managed his parents' portfolio of 70-plus student rental units. We lived in one of his rentals that was under renovation. It came time to move out, since the school year was starting, so I bought my first house in 2005. I managed to test most of the modern-day real estate buzz phrases with that one purchase: driving for dollars; house hacking; and buy, repair, rent, refinance, repeat.

The following year, a group of students knocked on the door mistakenly, as they had the wrong address. They were interested in renting the property, and I decided to rent it to them. In the mid-2000s, it was easy to get loans. Banks would practically throw money at you. I bought the two additional properties, and then I bought another one using an FHA loan.

Within a few years, I owned five units, mostly student housing. I was in my twenties, full of energy, and thought it was cool to learn how to do my own electric, plumbing, drywall, and flooring. I could repair and renovate everything under the roof.

Eventually, all the DIY work was catching up, and I was getting I burned out. I think this is why many real estate investors "top out" at five or six units. Only about 10 percent of investors grow beyond that, those who realize you need to leverage a team to scale and grow.

Then the economy crashed. At the time, the housing market was going down, but my 9-to-5 job was going up. I received a bunch of promotions, so I kept my eye on the money and focused on that. For the next five years, I didn't invest in any more properties.

Looking back, I regret that lull. A lot of investors who are rich and famous today got that way due to investing around 2011 and 2012. I missed that gold rush when the market was starting to roar back.

Robert: Did you learn on the go? Or were there investing books you read and recommend?
Phil: I read a lot of books. I read the entire *Rich Dad Poor Dad* series: *Cashflow Quadrant, ABCs of Real Estate Investing, etc.* I also read many landlording books (remember I was a DIY-aholic) such as *Landlording* and *The Landlord's Survival Guide*, by Jeffrey Taylor. Taylor's book is very helpful. I recommend it to anyone who owns rental properties—even if you don't ever want to manage them yourself or even answer calls.

Robert: The reality is that even if you have property managers, you still manage the property, right?
Phil: Yes. Everyone needs to be accountable at some point. I believe in rewarding tenants for good tenancy, which is beyond just paying rent on time. I give good tenants annual gifts such as gift cards.

Robert: Keeping tenants is essential. You are supplying the housing, but tenants have the money.
Phil: Turnovers are very expensive. I learned with the student

rentals as the tenants turned over every year. If people stay three to five years, instead of one to two years, you save a lot of money in things like advertising, cleaning, and renovating.

Robert: Who are the players on your investing team?
Phil: Investing is a team sport. It requires much more than collecting the rent and fixing stuff every now and again. You're running a business. I learned a lot the hard way. I was sued in the first six months of doing rentals and had to scramble to find a lawyer.

In the beginning, it can be more difficult and costly since you don't have the volume to realize any economies of scale. Since I was DIY or die, I had a hard time understanding the cost of contractors, and it does get expensive paying a handyman for random odds and ends. On the other hand, the hourly off-the-books guys can be cheaper, but highly unreliable and problematic (to say the least). For beginners, I suggest planning on this at first: Expect to pay for some lessons learned and do not waste too much time trying to cut costs.

Once you have more volume, it gets easier, and the load feels lighter. You gain leverage with the value provided to others. If you provide business, work, jobs, etc. you are helping them feed their families. As my business grew, I noticed I received more attention and response since they knew I had something more significant to provide. Also, your net worth grows over time, and you can leverage referrals to fill any gaps in services you need.

Today, I have a contractor who works for me full-time, and he has a part-time helper. I purposely keep them busy on renovations and so they're always available for maintenance calls. My contractor was an hourly employee who worked for another landlord. Ten years ago, he was a low-end maintenance guy doing painting, spackling, and some rougher maintenance work, not even much plumbing. But, we've grown together. He's fully licensed now, and he can do plumbing and electric.

Having volume helps. Being small is hard. I think that's why a lot of landlords burn out around five or six units because you're almost big enough to keep people busy, but you don't have enough work for them to be full-time. It can become a headache if you don't have somebody on staff. Even now, I'm probably still spending more than I might need to at times, but I'm building for the future.

Robert: What are your future plans?
Phil: My goal is to continue building the portfolio so I can support my family. Right now, I have a mix of single family and small multi-family units. This is what is most readily available in my local market. I have considered going the multi-family route and putting together syndications of 50-to-100-plus units.

From my professional work, I know a lot of high-net-worth folks who want to invest in real estate. They want to buy a big apartment building. But this is not a big multi-family area, and I'm not ready to expand into another market. I have a young family and a full-time job here. I want to be home with my kids. I don't want to travel to another area to manage multi-family units. I have one seven-unit property, a few two- and three-unit properties, and several singles.

Finding deals is tough in any market right now and my local market is quite competitive. There are a lot more buyers than sellers. Over the past few years, I have been building a marketing system to consistently bring in new deals. Since wholesalers are the ultimate deal finders, I've been studying and adapting many techniques used to wholesale properties. This is when you find a discounted property and contract an agreement, but you're able to assign the deal to someone else. You don't typically purchase the property yourself, but assign it to the end buyer for a fee.

Robert: How do you market your business?
Phil: I am building up Value Stream Properties as the main brand and investment vehicle. I have a web presence (valuestreamproperties.com) and create content for social media platforms and YouTube.

I also have We Buy Lehigh Valley Houses as a brand to find underdeveloped properties to fuel the investment vehicle. This was built out of necessity as finding deals became more difficult. The sheriff's sales were drying up. I don't see many for-sale-by-owner sales anymore.

To find new deals, I use a lot of different channels, including direct mail, cold calling, and texting.

The goal for this year is 40 units, and we are tracking nicely thus far. The plan for the next three years is to be well over 100 units and be established in another market as well.

CHAPTER 5

Key Skills

IN MY OPINION, real estate investing is not rocket science. The math isn't hard. Most fifth graders could do it. The concepts are easy to understand, and there are plenty of resources to read and people eager to help you learn.

Like anything in life, the right mindset will benefit you in real estate investing. I believe the right mindset includes:

- Become a continual learner.

- Let the numbers make your decisions.

- Always keep your promises.

Also, the right skills will serve you well in real estate investing. You need to be able to:

- Find deals.

- Analyze deals.

- Understand renovation and construction processes and costs.

- Learn how to finance your deals.

You do not need to be an expert at any of these to start. Reading the stories of the six investors in this book, you will learn that acting on what you know is better than trying to have a perfect understanding prior to acting.

The best training for your money that I know of is by April Crossley at lazygirlrei.com. Her no-nonsense—or no-BS—approach has helped her be successful. And, it has helped many other people succeed as well.

April Crossley

April flips houses, owns small multi-unit rentals, does some private money lending, and also has cutting-edge training videos on real estate investing. She is from Berks County, Pennsylvania, where she still invests, but she is currently traveling with her husband and Doberman named Georgia, in her RV while running her business remotely.

Robert: How did you get started in real estate?
April: It all started when I met my husband. He was a real estate agent, and I was working full time as a respiratory therapist. I had just begun studying for my master's degree.

One day on vacation, I picked up a book my husband was reading called *The One Minute Millionaire*. I was captivated by the stories of people living off the cash flow from their investments.

I grew up with the belief that you went to college, got a good job, retired when you were 65, and then you started to live your life. When I read *The One Minute Millionaire*, I thought, *This has to be a lie. There's no way people are going to live in your house and pay it off for you—and you keep the equity in it.*

I became a little obsessed with proving that the book was wrong, so I started educating myself on real estate investing. Then, my husband and I bought a house to flip. Next, we began buying rental properties. After that, we were buying rentals and flipping at the same time. We began building our portfolio.

We paused our buying for a bit when the market was crazy between 2005 and 2007. We bought most of our properties after the economic crash in 2009. In 2019, we started refinancing our houses and taking out big chunks of money in equity.

I had started to lose heart in the health-care industry. I saw so many patients not being treated well. In contrast, our new ventures in real estate were succeeding. By the time I was 35, we had flipped enough houses to replace my income. Now, we could show banks our track record of success and not need my 9-to-5 income to qualify for bank loans.

In 2013, I was ready to take the plunge. I left my health-care job, and I let my license lapse. In health care, once you do that, there's really no going back.

I thought it was going to be easy: I'd give up my full-time job, work for myself, and enjoy a relaxing life. It was great for a while, but I soon realized that I had simply created another job for myself. I was running my own flipping business, but I was even more stressed than when I worked for somebody else.

In one particularly dark moment, I told a friend, who's also a real estate investor, "I'm so stressed out. I'm not going to do this anymore. I think I'm just going to get a job as a secretary."

She referred me to a mentor, who helped me learn how to run my businesses like a business. Instead of working in my business, I learned how to work on my business. This helped me view my work more as a CEO, putting systems in place so that I could get out of my business.

When I was 39, my husband and I started snowbirding in Arizona. We bought an RV and lived in it for three months out of each year. We did that for a few years. Now I'm 42, and we just sold our house. We no longer have a permanent home. We travel the United States full time in our RV.

I'm still leading my investment business. I kick off each morning with a meeting with my team. My advice is that if you want to know if you work in your business or on your business, buy an RV. Go away for three months. If your businesses still keep running efficiently, then you work on your business. But, if your business can't run without you, you're too involved.

The first year, our three months away was very painful. But, I'm grateful because it showed us all the systems we were lacking and everything we didn't have in place. After we got home, we hired a bookkeeper and put other systems in place so that we could then leave again.

Robert: It forces you to think, right?
April: Painful situations force change. People are motivated by pain and fear. I was in pain. I said, "This is ridiculous. I want to enjoy my three months away, but I'm constantly getting phone calls." That's part of my journey.

Robert: I'm impressed by your training videos on finding deals and analyzing, rehabbing, estimating project costs, and financing deals. Could you share a little bit about these?
April: Those are the four keys to this business. You need to understand how to find deals, rehab, estimate the cost of projects, and finance deals. Early on, I found that many "experts" in real estate investing would just beat around the bush or not tell you the whole story. I wanted to help people and give them clear and direct information.

Robert: How do you find great deals?
April: Every deal we ever found was off-market. I'm a huge proponent of off-market deals. We look for properties that have code violations or are behind on taxes. With off-market deals, consistency with paperwork and details, such as properties with code violations, overdue taxes, or that are just empty or not being taken care of, and follow-up with

sellers is important. You'd be surprised at the number of sellers who call to say they want to sell, but then they won't call you back for months. You have to follow up with people and be consistent with mailings and contacts.

Robert: What key metrics do you use to analyze a deal?
April: I start with what the property is worth minus the profit I want to make, then minus the repair costs, closing cost to buy, and closing cost to sell. I aim to make at least $20,000 profit. A lot of people will do a deal for $10,000 or $15,000 profit. They don't understand that once you start ripping a house apart, if you find a major issue, which happens all the time, your profit will go right out the window. They end up making nothing.

Robert: Do you use bank mortgages or private lending?
April: There are people who have money, and it's sitting in a bank account making 0.5% interest or a retirement account they never look at or understand. We help people see real estate as a safe investment, as a way to diversify and earn 10% on the money they loan. The loan is secured by the property with a note and a mortgage. They wire the money to the settlement company. The borrower, or the flipper, uses that money to rehab the house, and they pay the private money lender back. Some of these private money lenders have $10,000 to $500,000 to lend, but they don't have the time to look for deals, nor the team to do the rehab, but they want to make a better return on their money.

Robert: How do you estimate how much money it will cost to rehab a property?

April: That's definitely difficult. The best way to figure it out is to ask a good contractor. Don't be afraid to pay them to give you their opinion on a potential house issue or a bid to do the repair. It's a nice idea to offer to send them pictures to save them a trip to come to see the property.

Another great way to learn is to walk through some homes with a home inspector. I did that one time, and it was super eye-opening. It was a great experience.

And finally, I often recommend that people just starting out in real estate investing who have little experience might want to enter into a joint venture with someone who has experience for their first few deals to learn the ropes.

April Crossley
april@lazygirlrei.com
YouTube: April Crossley
Facebook: Lazy Girl Real Estate Investing

Buy and Hold, Commercial Line of Credit, and Section 8

I have included this case study because it illustrates a different way to fund an investment and how you can use that investment to build relationships and help with other investment needs. Let me explain. One of the first hurdles new investors face is a lack of knowledge. The second hurdle is access to capital. It may seem surprising that I would list knowledge first and capital second. Both are important, but often people have capital, but they do not know how to access it or use it. Knowledge gives you facts and information—and the confidence to act.

One way to acquire both knowledge and capital is via a partnership. In this case study, I met another investor who seemed to have similar goals. We met at a real estate meetup. (See Chapter 4: Getting Started on page 43 to understand more.) I kept hearing from other more-experienced investors that finding deals was harder than finding money to buy them with. I wanted to believe them, but this seemed like a huge leap of faith.

The investor and I had dinner and a few conversations and decided if we could find a suitable investment, we would do this together, 50/50. We both had some money to invest. I liked to look for properties, him not so much. So, I began looking for a similar property as outlined in Case Study 1 (see page 35).

After a month of looking, we found a three-bedroom, one-bathroom row house that also had off-street parking— a garage. The house was in a little rougher shape, but acceptable to rent. It was in a little rougher area, but the city and big investors were making big strides in areas very close to this, so we felt that the area had promise.

What the house did not have was natural gas heat. The owner-investor was asking $50,000; we offered $45,000, and they accepted very quickly. We decided to use the proceeds from the first year's rent to pay for upgrading the heating system. So, our initial investment was:

Purchase price	$45,000
Upgrade heating *	$5,000
Other improvements	$3,000
Total Investment	$53,000

*This cost was eventually actually paid by the renter, because we saved our rent above our costs to make this very valuable upgrade to the property.

Cash Flow for Rental Analysis

Square feet	1,350
Monthly rent	$975.00
Property management (10%)	$97.50
Insurance	$60.00
Taxes	$165.00
Vacancy allowance (10%)	$97.50
Repairs allowance (10%)	$97.50
Total costs	$517.50
Net profit (47%)	$457.50

Unfortunately, this tenant left after one year, and, while they did not really damage the property, we were encouraged to put this property into the Section 8 program. This program allows low-income residents who qualify for the program to receive about 75% of the rent from county and state funds. Those funds come directly to the landlord, and the tenant pays the remainder. We did have to invest around $3,000 into it to meet their inspection requirements. The tenant and the property need to qualify each year to remain in the program. All this meant that we had not taken any profits from the property in more than a year.

I was reluctant to invest more of my capital from our retirement accounts, and we did not want to spend more of the limited cash flow from this property to make offers on new properties. We talked and determined to ask small local banks for two things: first to use the equity in this property (75% of the value or whatever they would agree to) and second to give us a line of credit that we could use to cover expenses that might come up while we were looking for other properties. Many said no, including where we had our checking account, but finally one bank said yes.

We were offered a $10,000 line of credit, and we could use the equity in this property as a down payment. This was a great lesson on three fronts. First, it showed us the power of leverage and using our equity to help us achieve our goals. Second, we came to understand more clearly how valuable our business is to the right bank. Banks need to lend money to make money, and we needed to see ourselves as valuable partners and business for them. Third, this cemented our partnership.

This property was producing a steady income for us, and by rethinking how to use it, we could move forward. There were more lessons. After a few months of looking, walking through quite a few off-market and other properties, we found a property with good potential to flip. We evaluated the ARV or retail sale price at $130,000. The investor-owner had wanted $85,000, but it had been lowered to $65,000 over a four-month period.

We went through the property with a construction professional I had used on my own house, and we paid him $100 to give us a detailed estimate. We also asked him if we could add a bathroom on the first floor. It had one on the second floor, but we knew that if we could add a second bathroom during our renovation, the value and thus the ease of selling would increase. We received a positive outcome on this and negotiated a sale price of $55,000. The details of this project will be outlined in Case Study 3 (see page 78). You will also see how the relationship we built with a commercial lender will help me in Case Study 4 (see page 89).

We kept this property rented for the next year and its cash flow paid for the holding costs; the insurance, utilities, taxes, and insurance for the new property we finished. While we did not take a lot of cash out of the property, we were able to use it to accomplish our goals. Now, we are planning on upgrading this property and selling it at retail in a couple months. We plan to use the proceeds, the appreciation in value, to upgrade the quality of our investments and probably upgrade to a multi-unit property.

Lessons Learned

- Partnerships multiply your options.

- You are an essential business to banks. Know it and act accordingly.

- There are many ways to tap the value in your property. Cash flow for income is only one.

CHAPTER 6

Investing Is a Team Sport

You MIGHT THINK that investing is a solitary activity: You find the property, secure a mortgage, fix up the house in your free time, resell it, then count your money. Popular HGTV shows perpetuate that myth with do-it-yourself hosts doing everything from house hunting, to tearing out walls, to fixing plumbing, to listing the house for sale.

My experience has been the opposite. In my business, I have assembled a team of truly talented people, including my accountant, Realtors, and contractors. These people make my job easy—and fun.

Here are two basic questions to ANY potential team member:

- As part of your work, do you work with investors?

- Do you or have you invested in real estate yourself?

If the answer is yes to both, ask for a few references. Check their references and find out if any of your existing contacts know them? Check your gut, do they feel like people you can trust?

You want people who will challenge your thinking at times. Having someone on your team to raise concerns about your strategies and actions is vital. You don't need cheerleaders.

Contractors: Sometimes the best are busy, and I mean *busy*. You need to be patient and *never* waste their time. I always pay for contractors to give me bids, at least until we have a strong working relationship. Usually $100 to $150 is sufficient. Remember to always get everything in writing when you decide to have them do the work. Walk away from people who demand high up-front fees. I normally do not give them more than one-third to start a job.

Realtors: A good Realtor is invaluable in my experience. They understand the markets they operate in. Good Realtors with investor experience earn their keep even more. *Never* waste their time. This means being clear about what you are looking for. When you make an appointment for a showing, always show up on time and be prepared. When you are not interested in a property, say so. When I am actively looking, I give them clear, designated times they can schedule showings. This is usually three to four hours, once or twice a week.

Lawyers: You cannot replicate the training and expertise of a good lawyer. You usually do not need one to file incorporation papers and other basic functions. But, for issues with government agencies, taxing authorities and some tenant issues, do not shy away from that expense. I spent more than $4,000 on a lawyer to help me handle the issues in Case Study 4 (see page 89). There is no way I could have handled this myself.

Accountants: I personally outsource all my bookkeeping. You may be able to do this and enjoy it. I do not. But, having good, reliable information from your books is essential in assisting you in making decisions. Having a reliable CPA to advise you on tax issues is critical as well. Like a good lawyer, an experienced CPA will more than pay for themselves.

Property managers: These are the folks who help you find and qualify tenants, collect rent, and handle the assignment of basic ongoing repairs and maintenance on your properties. They usually charge one month's rent to find, qualify, and place a tenant, and then 8% to 10% of the monthly rent they collect. These fees are somewhat negotiable. If you are investing remotely or out of state, this may be a critical factor.

Many people self-manage their properties until they grow to a certain level. Even if you choose to have a property manager, remember, you are still the owner and some oversight is still necessary. Regardless, even if you choose to self-manage, use these fees in your calculations. Your time is valuable and should be compensated.

Interview property managers before hiring them. Ask to see a sample of a report they provide their clients and if they deposit collected rents directly into your account. Ask them if they mark up any contractor fees or if you pay them directly. Find out if you can have set limits on what they can do on their own versus what you must approve. Get references and drive by some of the properties they manage. Finally, find out if they handle evictions? What are the costs involved?

You do not need to have every person on your team in place prior to acquiring your first property. Your team will grow as you need it to and as you grow, you may replace members of your team.

Steve Sell

Steve and his wife, Julie, are truly pioneers in the real estate industry, having started in 1980. They have done it all: flipping, wholesaling, holding rentals, training others, and now lending to others. They live in Lewes, Delaware, and his son runs his investment business.

Robert: How did you get into real estate?

Steve: I went to one of the earliest real estate seminars, a Lowry-Nickerson seminar, in 1981 in Washington, DC, which was run by Al Lowry. They had made a lot of money in real estate out on the West Coast. They were teaching people the art of flipping, syndicating, and holding.

I went to the seminar, and within two weeks, my wife and I bought our first house down in northern Virginia and got owner financing on it. We worked on it, fixed it up, and sold it about a year later. It was a real learning experience.

We just kind of kept going after that, just doing one after the other, one after the other, one after the other. It was just learning as you go. There was no internet at the time. The resources were really hard to come by in terms of planning houses and how you did everything. It was so different from how it is now.

Robert: How did you find some of your houses? You were just buying single-family homes through the 1980s?

Steve: Yes, we bought single-family homes. We did buy some multi-units, and we held some rentals early on. That wasn't something that appealed to me after going through it, so we just bought houses, renovated them, and sold them for years and years. Then, I developed a lot of marketing work. I was getting pretty good at finding houses at discounted prices. So, we started wholesaling: selling or assigning a deal to another investor or investors. The wholesaling led to financing them for other investors because, at the time, the houses we were buying weren't very expensive. We would cover the financing for six months, let the investors fix them up and sell them, and they would come back and buy another house with us, and we'd finance that house. The investor is paid back when the house sells.

Robert: You were a private money lender then?
Steve: Correct. Then, we just continued the process. Basically, anything that I could buy and renovate and sell myself, we would do that. Sometimes, we would have extra properties, and I would sell them to investors. We just kept going. It was one thing after the other, again and again and again, like baking cookies. You just keep repeating the same recipe over again.

Robert: What were some of the biggest challenges you faced early on?
Steve: There's a steep learning curve. Often contractors don't even know how much it costs to renovate a property. We frequently had cost overruns. If you get the budget wrong, you won't know for quite a while. When you do determine the actual costs, it will make the project either very exciting or very unexciting, depending on how it plays out.

Robert: When you were doing the wholesaling, I assume that was really less of a problem for you.
Steve: It was less of a problem. If you become a specialist in buying houses and buying at the right price, then it is just

much easier to flip them to another investor. In fact, that's what I used to call flipping, before anyone had invented the term *flipping* in the real estate business. We used to buy houses at 10 am and sell them at 2 pm to another investor. That was a flip. Anything under 24 hours was a flip. That's why the house flipping on TV didn't appeal to me, because I always thought flipping was something you did really quick. Buy it, flip it to another investor, make $20,000, that was a good day.

Robert: How did you find and connect with other investors?
Steve: My contractor became an investor. He saw what I was doing, so he wanted to buy houses and fix them up and sell them himself. I found houses for him, and he also began to find his own. He came to us to refinance, and we refinanced his deals for him. Along the way, we met other guys who were contractors, and they became investors. Later on, in the last 10 years, we gradually moved into the whole financing arena more than buying and selling real estate. Really, all you have to do is put a little word of mouth out there and say you have money available for real estate flipping, and the door begins to open. There are a lot of people out there doing that.

Robert: That's something that was hard for me to imagine at first.
Steve: Absolutely. The deal is all-important. If you can't find the deal, you have nothing. You can always find a partner who has money, who wants to participate and wants to do something with you, but if you don't have the deal, you don't have anything. We used to play around with partnerships. I used to offer a mentoring program for local real estate investors.

Robert: When were you doing these training programs?
Steve: I stopped doing them about three or four years ago. I

trained a lot of people, and they became borrowers, so then I financed a lot of their deals for them. But sometimes, people used to come to me and say, "Well, you know, I got this great deal, and I found a partner. He's got the money, and we're going to split it 60/40 or 50/50." They were giving all of their equity away just to get the money basically because they were grateful to find someone who would give them the money. But really, the deal is everything.

In the beginning, though, you don't have a lot of contacts. You don't know a lot of people with money, so you kind of take whatever you can get. It's like those guys who go in front of the sharks on *Shark Tank*. They're not sure what kind of a deal they can get, so a lot of times they'll take whatever deal is offered to them. They might give too much of the company away or whatever, but you learn from that. So, the next time around, you change and you learn from it, and go from there.

Robert: You are still financing deals then?
Steve: Yes. I had a company that evolved into hard money financing, and I recently retired. My son now owns that company, but we still finance a huge number of models every month.

Robert: You don't really own a lot of properties now?
Steve: I just sold my house that I lived in for 33 years in Pennsylvania about a month ago. I have a house down here in a little beach town. I also own a condo. But, when I was in the middle of doing real estate and fixing up houses, I usually owned about 15 houses at any one time. Three or four would be on the market for sale, and three or four or five would be getting renovated, and three or four would just be sitting, and some might be in the early acquisitions process. That's a lot of plates to juggle up in the air. That's a lot of work.

Robert: That is a lot of work! What do you find challenging about investing?

Steve: The math is easy, but the formulas are a little difficult. In the early years, no one wanted to share their formulas. It was all hush-hush. People would say, "I'm not telling you how I do things. Figure it out yourself." Then, the internet hit, and people were available online to teach you how to do it.

There were more people willing to teach you, but you couldn't really go buy a bunch of bank loan properties. I tried to buy bank-owned properties for years prior to 2009, but the banks wouldn't agree to sell anything, they did no discounts, and it was impossible. You couldn't buy houses that way. After 2009, if you needed a couple of projects, you would just go make 10 offers through your Realtor, and you'd probably buy two houses in two or three days. That went on for several years. And that's when all the real estate investing educators really got going.

Some programs charged $10,000 to $20,000 to teach you how to do real estate. I reviewed many courses, and I met a lot of people who spent that kind of money to take courses, but they still hadn't bought one house. Then we started working with them, mentoring them, and taking them through it step-by-step, but some of them were never going to buy a house.

You go out, put a bunch of offers on bank-owned properties, and you buy a few. But the problem is: That created thousands and thousands of new investors. So, then the prices went up, and all those properties are out there that people are trying to flip. Whereas before, you might buy a property and get $30,000 to $50,000 for turning the property over.

It got to the point where the competition was so stiff, most guys were lucky to make $10,000 to $15,000. And then their numbers were based on that $10,00 to $15,000 and they'd run into a problem doing the project, and they'd lose $5,000, or they'd end up doing it for nothing. Well, that was a learning experience. So that's been the problem in the last five years; there's so much competition that it drives the prices of the inventory up, and it's hard for people to find anything that works. Good deals are still out there, though.

Robert: Can you speak about the competitive real estate landscape in the area, considering investors from New York and New Jersey seem to be getting involved.
Steve: With interest rates so low, people are trying to put their cash anywhere they can to make money. But I think a lot of times, a lot of those guys who are buying are agents for the investors. I don't think they know the business as well as they should. They're buying properties that I don't think are going to work out, but nobody's going to know for a while. Their investors are not going to be too unhappy for a while, and then later, they will be, or it won't work out. But where are they going to put their money?

Robert: Were you ever a landlord and actually collected rent?
Steve: Early on I was. We bought a triplex and my wife and I renovated it and put tenants in. It was really a hassle. We had a really nice property, but it was in an area where they had some break-ins, and eventually we lost our really good tenants. Looking for new tenants can be really challenging.

The triplex was an experiment because when I had taken the real estate investment course, they always said you want to focus on single-family homes, which appreciate faster. They're a little harder to manage, but you can do single-family homes or you can do units. If you get a bunch of units, then they're easier to manage, but they don't appreciate as much. So, I thought, *Okay, this is my education. I'll buy this triplex and try it.* We tried it, and you end up leaving your money in it. Of course, when you're starting out, you don't have a lot of cash, so if you leave your cash in a project, then you don't have any cash or working capital to go somewhere else. The tenants were a problem, so I kind of abandoned that.

Later on, I started doing single-family home rentals. We did about 10, and they worked well. We bought the properties really cheap, fixed them up (they looked really nice), put tenants in, the tenants were there for about five years, but the tenants really damaged them, so we sold them all in five years. That was a good experiment. At that point, I just started buying, renovating, and selling. Everybody's different, people do different things, but I was comfortable with that. I had some experience with property management people that was really awful. They were constantly putting tenants in, getting them out, charging you to get them in, charging you to get them out, and so on. So, instead, I actually have a farm right now that has three houses on it, and I've got tenants in there. They've been there five or six years, and I get checks every month in a really timely fashion. It's nice. But it wasn't something I planned. It was a property I bought to subdivide, and it still has three houses on it.

Robert: Some seasoned people I know have gone into syndications, such as big apartment buildings, with either general or limited apartments. Did you ever look into that or do anything like that?
Steve: I haven't done any of that. I looked into that early on in my career. I read a whole limited partnership agreement one time from some big company, and I saw how they were making money hand over fist. They promoted it as a great way to own something. But I never did it. I did syndications with other investors where I created limited partnerships, and they put up money, and I went out and bought and sold properties

and did subdivisions and bought farmland. I did some things like that, but never any apartment buildings. I just never really got into that. It probably would have been good if I could have done that, but you get into a comfortable zone, and you just keep doing it. In my case, buying single-family homes was really easy, not very risky, and every time, we made a little bit of money. After a while, it added up, and we had to lend some money. It just became comfortable.

Robert: If you had to give advice to somebody who was starting out, what would you tell them to do?
Steve: Real estate is one of those things where, when you're young and you have a lot of energy and you're full of enthusiasm, you just dive into it. So, you make a lot of mistakes, but you learn. Right now, there are so many people getting into the real estate business who do the same thing—they're excited, so they want to quit their jobs and do it full time. My piece of advice would be don't quit your job and jump into real estate full time. Keep it on the sideline, and it will be a really exciting sideline way to make some money. But, don't quit your long-term job where you're going to get your pension and your retirement.

You have to be the kind of person who's flexible enough to learn from mistakes. And hopefully, you don't make too big of a mistake. Because the big mistakes are the ones that wipe you out, and then you don't ever go out and buy another house. You can make some small mistakes and learn.

I also think it's wise to find a mentor. The program they had here in Delaware gave people an opportunity to learn, and they got to work with other investors. They could ask people how they did things. If they had a problem or question, they could call up their coach and say, "Hey, my tenants left in the middle of the night. What do I do?" or "My tenants don't pay their rent. What do I do?" or "The contractor took all my money and left town. What do I do?" So, at least you have someone to talk to who's had some experience to help you get through things. I think it's a good idea to have some kind of group that you're working with or a group of investors that you can talk to.

I was mostly on my own for all those years. My wife helped me a lot. She was really great. She jumped in and helped me with many issues. She became my acquisitions specialist in sheriff's sales. Sometimes, she'd get in the car and we'd look at 20 houses on Monday, 20 houses on Tuesday, and 20 houses on Thursday, and then we'd go to the sheriff's sale the next Tuesday and bid on 60 houses. Maybe we'd buy one, maybe we'd buy three, maybe we didn't buy any. But every month, it was really a lot of work to check them all out and try to estimate what kind of fix-up they needed, because we couldn't walk inside. That's a real interesting part of the business.

Robert: Now your son is running your finance company?
Steve: Yes. My son does a lot of flips himself. He's a Realtor, and he runs the finance team. He's really into it. He's really, really busy. I'm happy to be out of it. I had almost 40 years of it.

I know one of the things you wanted to discuss was the process of building a team. But, back when I was working, both my strength and my weakness was that I liked to work alone, because I liked to be able to count on whomever I worked with. I know if I work with myself, if I want to get something done, I'll get it done.

But, on the other hand, I think my weakness is that I like to work by myself. As a result, maybe my business could have been multiplied, or I could have done bigger things if I had relied more on other people.

My wife definitely helped me a lot. She helped buy a lot of

properties, managed things, and took care of the accounting and bookkeeping. She was always really positive and supportive, and she never criticized me. She was amazing. Somebody said, "Behind every successful man, there's a woman that's not impressed."

Robert: They know the truth. What sort of people were on your team, and what did they bring to the table?
Steve: I had an attorney, of course. You need an attorney who's flexible. He was a great guy. And you have to find people like that who are working outside the box. All these established attorneys, you send them a deal and they want to schedule it three weeks out. Like, no, you need to find somebody who is ready to work with you. You bring so much business to the attorney. Not only did I bring my own business to the attorney, but I would take all my buyers to him.

For years and years, I sublet my own houses; I never hired Realtors. I would just take them back to the same attorney. He would do all the paperwork, and then he would gain 50 new clients a year. The same thing with our real estate loans. The attorney was important. He was sharp and would work with you that way, and I think there are a lot of attorneys who would do that. I don't think it's hard to find somebody like that. After all, they want to build their business, too.

I also hired a lot of accountants early on. I would say you don't need an accountant on your team as much as you need a good tax adviser. You need somebody to give you advice on how to minimize taxes.

What other people were on my team? Contractors, that's a tough one. I liked to hire guys who were their own bosses. I liked the handyman type who did a little bit of everything. If there was a plumbing problem, he could fix it. If there was an electrical problem, he could fix it. He could put a kitchen in, and he could put a bathroom in. I liked that kind of guy who could do anything, and he worked for himself, so his overhead was low. As soon as you hire a big company, they have all sorts of overhead—retirement plans, vacation bonuses, all sort of things. So, suddenly, it costs twice as much to use them.

A lot of times, I hired guys and worked with them, training them and helping them get started. Then, they would be good for four or five years, and then they'd get to the point where they had so much experience and were doing so well that, inevitably, they'd quit and go out on their own. That happened several times—which, good for them. They want to better their situations.

A Flip with Other People's Money

After my partner and I purchased the property outlined in Case Study 2 (see page 60), we began looking for other properties to purchase, initially to rent, but also perhaps to buy, repair, and resell, or flip. The immediate area in the Lehigh Valley where we lived and had acquired properties individually and together was becoming more competitive. We decided to look a little north. We had some of the key team members in place. I had met a good Realtor there and a potentially good property manager. I also knew a construction professional in the area.

I was looking at bank-owned properties. You can learn about them from your Realtor or find them on MLS or sites like zillow.com. Our Realtor also showed us properties. Plus, I always am looking for what is known in the industry as driving for dollars. This simply means being aware of properties that may be listed as for sale by owner, look abandoned, have been listed on the MLS for a long time, or have had their price lowered quickly over a two- to three-month period.

We finally found a property to consider. It was in the small Pennsylvania town of Jim Thorpe. I had noticed the asking price was decreasing—rapidly. I asked my Realtor to show it to me. The owner had been doing his own home renovations—badly. He wanted to get out of the property, so we negotiated a decent price.

Initial Sale Analysis

Square feet	1,568
After Repair Value	$134,900
Property purchase	$ 55,000
Other purchase costs	$ 1,350
Renovation costs	$40,000
Total purchase costs	$96,350

Holding Costs

(In general, you should aim to turn a property in six months.)

Insurance (6 months)	$ 360
Taxes (6 months)	$ 1,800
Utilities (6 months)	$ 600
Total holding costs	$ 2,760

Sale Costs

Commission (6%)	$8,100
Other closing costs	$850
Private money	$7,000
Total selling costs	$15,950
Total costs	$115,060
Projected profit (14.7%)	$19,840

Actual Sale Analysis

Square feet	1,568
After Repair Value	$130,000
Property purchase	$55,000
Other purchase costs	$1,350
Renovation costs	$47,000
Total purchase costs	$102,350

Holding Costs

(This house took us 14 months to sell.)

Insurance (14 months)	$840
Taxes (14 months)	$4,200
Utilities (14 months)	$1,400
Total holding costs	$6,440

Sale Costs

Commission (5%)	$6,500
Other closing costs	$850
Private money	$9,000
Total selling costs	$16,350
Total costs	$124,040
Projected profit (6.8%)	$6,980

Because we had a rented property, the holding costs were covered by that, so this did not affect our cash flow during the project. Also, our private money lender agreed to take a little less than they might have earned. We changed Realtors, and our new agent graciously accepted a 5% commission instead of 6%. The roughly $6,440 was actually paid to us at closing, but an accurate assessment of this project is mediocre.

We took much longer to sell the property, missed the ARV by $4,900, and had higher renovation costs than projected. In the end, this was a low-profit project, but it was a great learning experience.

Looking back, we took too long to finish the renovations. We brought it onto the market in October. When it did not sell by Christmas, we took it off the market until April and then sold it fairly quickly. In all, it took us 14 months from acquisition to sale, much too long.

Lessons Learned

- Missing ARVs, timelines, and budgets impacts your bottom line. Pay attention.

- You need reserve funds and options. Luckily, we had a line of credit and cash flow from another property. If you don't have that, you need cash.

- Nourish partnerships with your Realtor, contractor, lenders, and financial partners with communication and transparency.

- This project was funded 100% with private money. I found the project and our construction partner, but I did not invest any of my own money into this project. The private money lender now wants me to find other deals for him.

- Even though we did not meet all of our goals, it was a great learning project. Going forward, we are in a position to do better next time.

CHAPTER 7

More Words of Wisdom

THERE'S ANOTHER WAY to invest in real estate that people might not think of. Yet, it's a very practical, low-barrier-to-entry way to get started—and to own property in your favorite vacation location to boot! You can buy property and rent it, such as on Airbnb or Vrbo. But you need to approach this as a business. Appropriate due diligence and team members are essential.

Partnerships are also a great way to get started. You may have money or need it. You may be able to provide a service that others can not. The deal itself may dictate that. As with any relationship, transparency and clear, regular communication are essential. Trust is the coin of the realm. And, partnerships do not need to last forever. They could be for one deal for a particular type of project like flips or for a geographic area. Use a lawyer as appropriate here.

A hurdle some people have is relationships with banks. They are used to the idea that you need banks, and that they are a kind of gatekeeper. This is not false, especially when you are trying to purchase your first home to live in. As an investor, however, banks need you as much as you need them. They make their income by lending. So, without you, the investor, they have no income. One thing I did early on was to scan all my tax returns and other relevant information onto a thumb drive and label them clearly. This allowed me to always have what banks and anyone else really that needed it quickly and accurately.

And banks are not your primary source of funds. Private money lenders are people who have money to lend on a short-term or deal basis. Hard money lenders are professional private money lenders. Their fees are usually higher but can still be valuable. There is a lot to be said and learned on this and is beyond the scope of this book or discussion. Please refer to some of the books in the Resources and References (see page 100).

Relationships are everything, in a way. They allow you to multiply what you do. Keeping your word, clear communication, and always being on time are basics. Be careful about expecting too much from a relationship, until you have had sufficient time and experience with them. Good ones take time.

Julia Okamoto

Julia did not start investing in real estate until later in life, even though she was always interested. Her investments suit her and her husband's goals perfectly. They provide monthly income in retirement, and the equity in their properties allowed them to purchase a business for her husband that their son now operates. She lives in New York state with her family, though her real estate investments are in Pennsylvania.

Robert: What motivated you to get into real estate?

Julia: I've always been interested in real estate, and I wanted to invest in it because I always believed that it was a great way to make residual income. I like real estate, and I actually like looking at houses. For me, looking at a house is not a chore at all; it's a fun thing to do. At my age now, I don't want to do things that aren't enjoyable and fun. But, I was never able to get involved in it in the past. My husband and I discussed it at certain times, but it was never the right time.

We kind of fell into real estate investing when my husband's job moved to Pennsylvania. So, we thought, "Guess we have to go live in Pennsylvania now." My husband and I looked for a house, but when we came back and told our kids, who were older at the time, they said, "We're not moving. We don't want to move to Pennsylvania. What's in Pennsylvania? There's nothing there."

We actually had a house in mind to buy that was around $200,000, which we thought would be great. If we sold our then-current house for $400,000, we'd be in good shape, but after the kids responded that way, we started to rethink. I told my husband that I didn't want to go to Pennsylvania if the kids didn't want to go, and I wasn't going without them. So, we kind of changed our focus and looked for something smaller that David could stay in a few days a week. So, that's kind of how we started. We bought a small house and ended up renting it out because as it turned out my husband didn't have to relocate as quickly as he originally thought. We kind of liked that idea. We saw the opportunities in the Poconos for real estate investing.

Robert: So you looked at Pennsylvania as an inexpensive market?
Julia: It was way cheaper, and someone said it's the foreclosure capital of the world in that area.

Robert: Yes, banks loaned people money early on in 2008, 2010, maybe before that. They loaned so much money, much more than the properties were worth. They did a lot of building, too, and then the market just crashed. So a lot of people just lost their houses.
Julia: We focused on foreclosures at that time and found one. It was really run-down, like animals had been living there. It stunk; it was terrible. Anyway, it was really cheap, $67,000 for a fairly large three-bedroom house. Exactly at that time we received a gift of money from my husband's parents. That helped. We bought the house, fixed it up, and were planning to live there, or live in the other one if the tenant left. Either way, we would have one to rent and one to live in. We then looked for another one, and we bought another one. We bought only three houses. We're not big real estate moguls or anything like that. All are in the Milford area.

The third house we bought was in Dingmans' Ferry, in a planned community. That wasn't a foreclosure. After that purchase, we stopped for a while. A couple years passed, and it turned out that David was going to leave his job. We later bought a business in California, so that really took up all our available capital.

Having those properties helped us to buy the business that we bought in California. The equity in our properties allowed us to purchase the company.

Robert: Did you read any books that helped you?
Julia: I did way back before I got involved in this. But I've always remembered those books. I read *Rich Dad, Poor Dad.* And back in the 1980s there was a popular program going around called *No Money Down.* I didn't buy into it, but a friend of mine did. She had a manual that I looked at, but I didn't get involved. *No Money Down* just sounded too risky to me. I think that's how we ended up with a lot of those foreclosures.

Robert: I guess your husband's running the business?
Julia: He's not running the day-to-day. He's like a chairman. When they want to move forward, he gets involved. He tries to find ways to make the business more profitable. My son reports the numbers to him every day.

Our real estate investments have given us more flexibility and time, which are similar, and of course more money, so we have more choices in life. We can travel more. It is residual income that comes even when we're not doing anything. We're making money while we sleep, as they say.

Robert: Do you have any advice for people who are thinking about getting into real estate?
Julia: There is a lot to learn. Even if someone else is doing all the heavy lifting, you still have to keep an eye on what's going on. For example, we went to one house we were restoring, and

the workers had put a big hole in the hardwood floor. They were trying to hide it. But we found it and made them fix it; we made sure they took that plank out and put another one in. You have to watch the work, because not everyone is reliable.

Robert: Do you have any other advice you'd give people?
Julia: I think if someone really has a desire to do it, I would say go ahead. But just learn as much as you can first. Make sure you have the money to invest. I think you have to take some chances, but, especially if people are older, I wouldn't advise them to take too big a chance and put all their savings into it.

I also think people have to know *why they're doing it.* And if they're thinking that they're going to rent out something, then they have to ask themselves if they want to be a landlord, and if they're prepared to deal with all the hassles that come with being a landlord. Can they handle all the issues that come up? If they say yes, that's okay, I'm fine with that. I think people have to look at their motivation, too, because if they just think, *Oh, I'm going to get rich*, that may not be the case, and I don't really think that's a good motivation.

Robert: You had some of your homes as vacation rentals, right?
Julia: Yes, we did. We did Airbnb for about three years. That worked out well for my husband's situation. He worked near Milford five days a week, and we kept our house in New York. We used to go there and stay; I'd go with him two or three days a week, and then I'd come back to New York. It wasn't that far to commute, an hour and a half, but still if you do it every day, it's exhausting. We would offer our house in Pennsylvania via Airbnb on the weekends or whenever we weren't there. That worked well for us, because the Airbnb

money was better than monthly rent. We made pretty much the same money doing Airbnb on weekends as we would have made renting. But in the summer, we could rent it out for $2,000 a week!

At one point in time, we offered all three houses as Airbnb rentals, in between tenants. That's a good thing to keep in mind if you have a rental: If you're in between tenants, or you haven't rented it yet, you can join one of the vacation rental apps.

Robert: You have Vrbo and Airbnb?
Julia: Yes, we did both Vrbo and Airbnb. You get different clients from each one. With Airbnb, you usually get a "couple of nights" type of people. With Vrbo, the clients are more long-term.

Sheriff's Sale

When I saw that the other side of the duplex my wife and I own was to be sold at a sheriff's sale, I knew we had to buy it. A sheriff's sale is a public auction at which property that has been defaulted on is repossessed. The proceeds from the sale are used to pay the sheriff the costs to sell the property, municipal liens, city and school district taxes, and then other people owed money, such as contractors. Finally, the mortgage lenders and banks are paid. A property is sold via sheriff's sale when the lender or lien holders—such as the school district, city, and even contractors—have given up trying to work out repayment arrangements with the owner. It is always a sad tale, and often the property is in bad shape. Both were true in this case. I chose to include this case study and Case Study 3 (see page 78) to be honest and show that the *real business of investing is not at all like the TV shows.*

Although I had attended a few sheriff's sales before as a spectator and knew the basics of how they worked, I knew that I needed to nail down the specifics of every step and be ready before I went to this one.

First, I called the attorney representing the lender and inquired when they would know their bottom-line amount they would accept. Yes, they will tell you this, but only a week or so before the sale. I paid $150 for a title search on the property, which included all the lien holders on the title. There were quite a few. I didn't pay for title insurance, only the title search because I could save another $800 to $1,000 at that time. I didn't need it to be insured. I only needed to see what liens were on the title.

Next, I paid $400 to a lawyer who specializes in real

estate law to make sure I understood the sheriff's sale process correctly and to obtain his advice on this sale specifically. I got permission to walk through the property with a contractor to get his rough estimate on renovation costs. Finally, I met with my commercial lender to obtain his pre-approval on his financing the purchase, including the renovation costs, with me putting 20% down.

In this county, the sheriff's sale rules are that you have to pay 10% of the price you bid with a certified bank check at that time. So, I had to determine what I was willing to pay and get a certified check for 10% of that amount. A week prior to the sale, I confirmed that their bottom-line price was $67,400. I was willing to pay $70,000 for this property, so I went to the sale with a certified check for $7,000.

The day of the sale, November 23, 2019, was fairly uneventful. Only one other person bid on the property, and only briefly. I won the bid for $67,700, paid the clerk with my check, and was given a receipt and a letter of what to expect next. I had 30 days to pay the total amount due. With that receipt and additional money to equal 10% of the purchase price, my commercial lender paid for the property in full on December 3, 2019. Soon after, I found out from the sheriff's office that I would likely not receive the actual title to the property until mid-January 2020. It turned out to be January 31; the administrative process takes that long.

In the meantime, I was informed by the current resident that they had obtained a legal aid attorney and likely would not be out of the property until July or August! I won't go into all the issues and problems this family had, but drug addiction was at the center of it. And of course, the COVID-19 pandemic hit in March of that year as well.

I contacted my attorney, who advised me to bring an ejection motion against the previous owners. This is somewhat different than eviction. We did so, but in the meantime, the COVID crisis had basically closed all the courts. In the end, we negotiated a settlement for them to leave the property on April 15, with a small payment as an incentive. My legal fees cost me more than $4,000.

Am I discouraging you from investing in real estate yet? I hope not, but sheriff's sales are not the place to start. I would not have done this, except I already owned the other side and I wanted to control who moved in there. And I knew I could increase the value of both by owning both sides of the duplex. I pressed on, taking the long view.

When we obtained possession of the property, the COVID lockdown was in full effect. Most construction activities were prohibited, and materials were hard to get because so many homebound people were doing remodeling. Supply chains everywhere were disrupted. We persevered and began in earnest around May 1. I had hoped to be done by then! We lost probably six weeks of time throughout the summer waiting for materials. We finished the renovation about September 15 and had it rented by October 15. Luckily, I have a good relationship with my commercial lender, who allowed me to pay interest only on my borrowed money until the home was rented and I had income on it. My construction guy was a gem and worked with me and around all the delays and problems. Relationships and trust count in this business—as in all aspects of life.

Here is a rough summary of the costs of this project. If this property had not been next to one I already owned, I would not have purchased this.

Purchase Analysis

After Repair Value	$135,000
Property purchase	$67,700
Pre-purchase costs	$1,100
Legal costs	$4,400
Renovation	$51,000
Closing costs on loan	$2,100
Total	$126,300

Rent Analysis

Monthly rent	$1,200
Mortgage (20-year commercial loan)	$711
Taxes	$160
Insurance	$50
Vacancy allowance (10%)	$120
Repairs allowance (10%)	$120
Total expenses	$1,161
Profit (3.25%)	$39

Still, how many businesses operate with similar profit margins? More than you might know. And with the benefits of depreciation, a unique aspect of real estate, this project will turn out fine. I would not encourage anyone to pursue a sheriff's sale or similar project without significant experience and some resources. Also, because the house was basically rebuilt, it should have few maintenance problems.

These are slim margins, but my tenant is paying for all these costs, and an upside to all this is that now I own both sides of the property. The value of my previously owned side went up 10%, or around $16,000 just by fixing up the other side. Another bonus with this project is we now have a potential building site that we can develop, which is probably worth $35,000.

Lessons Learned

- Due diligence, a solid team of advisors, four plus years of experience, and having some financial reserves were crucial.
- Patience is truly a virtue, and keeping the long view in focus keeps you inspired.
- This may be my most profitable investment yet, in the long term.
- Do not use sheriff's sales unless you have to.

CHAPTER 8

Key Real Estate Formulas

THERE ARE MANY FORMULAS used in the real estate investment world. As you use these tools, you'll become more familiar and more comfortable with them. This is not geometry, algebra, or calculus. It is addition, subtraction, multiplication, and division.

Rent per Square Foot

Equation: Rent per square foot
= gross rent / square footage of property

This metric is used when comparing investment properties. You will see this on all property listings.

Price-to-Rent Ratio

The price-to-rent ratio is the purchase price of the property divided by the amount of rent you expect to receive each year before expenses.

Equation: Price-to-rent ratio
= price of property / Annual rental revenue

This formula creates a useful metric between comparable properties to determine which presents a better value to the investor.

Year One Cash-on-Cash Return

Year one cash-on-cash return compares the rental cash flow in year one to the initial cash investment in the property in year one. This calculation, where year one cash flow gets divided by the initial cash investment, is called the year one cash on cash return.

Equation: Year one cash-on-cash return
= cash flow / year one capital expenses

You can think of this as comparing this use of cash to others.

Break-Even Ratio

The break-even ratio is sometimes also called the break-even occupancy ratio. It is the sum of annual operating expenses and mortgage expenses divided by projected yearly rental income.

Equation: Break-even ratio
= (total annual operating expenses
+ total annual mortgage expenses)
/ projected annual rental income

Dividing these expenses by the projected rental income will tell you what proportion of the property must get rented out to break even.

Net Operating Income

Net operating income is calculated by taking total revenue from gross rents and subtracting all operating expenses, such as maintenance and vacancy allowance. But it excludes capital items such as principal and interest payments and depreciation expense.

Equation: Net operating income
= total revenue from gross rents – total operating expenses

Debt Service Coverage Ratio

The debt service coverage ratio (DSCR) measures the rental income against the debt payments from the mortgage.

Equation: Debt service coverage ratio
= net operating income / total annual mortgage expenses

This measures how much of a cushion there is between the income and the mortgage payment.

Loan-to-Value Ratio

The loan-to-value ratio is used to calculate the amount of debt someone has relative to the value of their property.

Equation: Loan-to-value
= outstanding debt / value of property

The lower the ratio, the better, in terms of having less debt relative to the asset.

Capitalization Rate

This calculation, also called CAP rate, is a crowd favorite in the world of real estate. That is because it is a fairly quick and easy way to compare two rental properties. All you need to do to calculate this is estimate your net operating income. Or, if it is ownership in an existing property, use actual numbers to calculate net operating income. Then divide net operating income by the property value.

Equation: Capitalization rate
= net operating income / value of property

It's also useful to be able to track trends in the rental market as many investors follow this metric.

CHAPTER 9

Find Your *Why*

BY NOW, YOU KNOW that real estate investing is not a walk in the park, but it provides tremendous opportunities to build real wealth, offers a path to financial independence, and offers a unique method to diversify your existing investments even if being an active investor is not for you.

If you have skipped over the investor interviews in this book, go back and read them before moving on. There is so much experience and wisdom shared there that it's impossible to overestimate their value. So, why do I now want to talk about a soft subject like purpose, and what in the world is internal capital?

Investing in real estate will require you to learn about the building and renovation of buildings, financial analysis, and banking and finance. It will help you to grow in your ability to form teams, manage them, and produce results. You will not be required to be an expert in any of these areas, but you need to know enough to hire, manage, and evaluate people who are.

You do not need to build an empire of thousands of units, but you could. For all these reasons, defining why you are doing this is vitally important. Consider the following quote:

> *Compare yourself to yourself yesterday, not to younger people who aren't you. Everyone progresses at a different rate, so don't let anyone else make you feel behind. You probably don't even know exactly where you are going, so feeling behind doesn't help.*

Approach your own personal voyage and projects like Michelangelo approached a block of marble, willing to learn and adjust as you go, and even to abandon a previous goal and change directions entirely should the need arise.

—From *Range* by David Epstein

As you research real estate investing, you'll hear a lot about financial freedom.

First, there is no freedom outside of your core values and principles—your *why*. Your purpose could be to leave your 9-to-5 job. It could be to invest on the side as you continue to work or even after you retire. Think of a ship readying to sail: Determining your destination is important. Isn't it? Your core values are the rudder that allow you to steer your ship and maintain control. Your destination can change, or you can have more than one, but you need to have one. And determining why you are sailing is essential. But also, your values, how you steer your ship as you sail, are important as well. Honesty, trust, diligence, and a willingness to learn from failures are good ones to start with. What others would you add?

Second, there is no freedom without responsibility. I remember the story of a young man who complained to his parents and teachers about all the rules and expectations placed upon him. His response was to join the Army. I'm sure you can guess how that worked out. He thought this would give him freedom, but before he could have any freedom within this new system, he would have to learn an entire new level of responsibility. If we want freedom, financial and otherwise, we need to take responsibility for our actions.

Third, there is no freedom without results. In life, effort is not enough, nor are ideas. You have to endeavor to sail your ship to its destination, using the tools of your purpose and core values to get you there. You had to learn how to win and how to lose growing up. Your results in life apply to investing in real estate and any other activity. When you learn from your wins and losses, it provides a compounding effect. Just as small deposits of money earn interest over long periods of time, so do our actions.

What powers your journey is tapping into your internal capital. As an investor, you know that using your monetary capital to invest in properties that can provide cash flow, appreciation, equity, and leverage provides almost unlimited power. Learning how to use them determines everything.

Your internal capital is your inner resources. These include your confidence, knowledge, and unique experiences in life. This could include your faith tradition. It is the ability to find hope when faced with difficulty. It is the ability to learn from failures, to get up and start again. It is the ability to cultivate gratitude as a daily mindset, something you choose each morning and end each day with. I want to leave you with my favorite prose—words that have always remained valuable to me:

> *Gratitude unlocks the fullness of life. It turns what we have into enough, and more. It turns denial into acceptance, chaos to order, confusion to clarity. It can turn a meal into a feast, a house into a home, a stranger into a friend. It turns problems into gifts, failures into successes, the unexpected into perfect timing, and mistakes into important events. It can turn an existence into a real life, and disconnected situations into important and beneficial lessons. Gratitude makes sense of our past, brings peace for today, and creates a vision for tomorrow.*

> **—Melody Beattie**

RESOURCES AND REFERENCES

Becker, Bill. *On the Brink of Bankruptcy: Discovering the Power Within*

First Edition, 2008

"This powerful and inspiring work—part autobiography, part manual for living—describes Bill's rise from the tough streets of Philadelphia through careers in electrical contracting, politics, and real estate."

Bloom, Bryan S., CPA. *Confessions of a CPA: The Truth about Life Insurance*

First Edition, 2013

"A question I get every day is, 'Why isn't everyone implementing the principles in this book?' The answer to that question is that everyone who understands these financial truths is implementing them. There is a finite amount of information that humans know about the universe. All this known information falls into three categories. First, there is a certain amount of information we know and that we are aware that we know. Second, there is a large amount of information that we know nothing about. We know that there are certain fields or concepts 'out there,' but we really don't know anything about them. The third category of knowledge represents information we don't know, and we're not even aware that we don't know it."

Cook, Steve. *Lifeonaire: An Uncommon Approach to Wealth, Success, and Prosperity*

First Edition, 2018

"Will becoming a millionaire really set you free? How about the American Dream? If we, as a nation, declare freedom to be our number-one priority, then why do so many of us, at a gut level, feel less freedom than ever? Americans are working harder than ever to obtain financial *success and material possessions based on the delusion that more will lead to a better life. The typical American is trading away the vast majority of their life in hopes that, someday, they will have enough to experience 'the good life.'"*

Faircloth, Matt. *Raising Private Capital: Building Your Real Estate Empire Using Other People's Money*

First Edition, 2018

"Are you ready to help other investors build their wealth while you build your real estate empire? The roadmap outlined in this book helps investors looking to inject more private capital into their business—the most effective strategy for growth! Author and real estate investor Matt Faircloth helps you learn how to develop long-term wealth from his valuable lessons and experiences in real estate. Get the truth beyond the wins and losses from someone who has experienced it all."

Ferguson, Mark. *Build a Rental Property Empire: The No-Nonsense Book on Finding Deals, Financing the Right Way, and Managing Wisely*

Third Edition, 2017

"This book gives you everything you need to know about rental proper-ties. From basic fundamentals to advanced strategies for buying with little money down and financing many properties. Mark Ferguson has been a successful real estate investor and real estate agent since he graduated from college in 2001. He has bought well over 100 houses in his career and sold over 1,000 houses as a real estate agent. Mark loves to write in a no-nonsense, easy-to-read manner that delivers as much information as possible in the shortest amount of time."

Kiyosaki, Robert T. *Rich Dad, Poor Dad: That the Rich Teach Their Kids about Money That the Poor and Middle Class Do Not!*

20th Anniversary Edition, 2017

"The main reason people struggle financially is because they have spent years in school but have learned nothing about money. The result is that people learn to work for money, but never learn to have money work for them."

Kiyosaki, Robert T. *Rich Dad's Guide to Investing: What the Rich Invest in, That the Poor and the Middle Class Do Not!*

First Edition, 2000

"Investing means different things to different people. In fact, there are different investments for the rich, poor and middle class. Rich Dad's Guide to Investing *is a long-term guide for anyone wo wants to become a rich investor and invest in what the rich invest in. As the title states, it is a 'guide' and offers no guarantees . . . only guidance."*

Lassiter-Lyons, Susan. *Getting the Money: How to Raise $250,000 in Private Money in the Next 30 Days*

First Edition, 2015

"Real estate investing is a proven wealth builder, but it can be a challenge to get started without a money tree in your backyard . . . at least until today. When you read Getting the Money, *you'll discover a simple framework to raise private capital for real estate, the three types of private investors and how to approach each of them, how to close deals . . . and make the process fun and profitable."*

Leroux, David. *Unleash Your Airbnb Revenue: How to Make the Most Money on Your First Airbnb Listing*

First Edition, 2018

"The author and his wife have made tens of thousands in the last three years with over 100 five-star reviews on our average suburban home, and I want to give you the best chance to do the same."

McLean, Michael and Cipriano, Nick. *Section 8 Bible: How to Invest in Low-Income Housing*

Second Edition, 2019

"Renting to Section 8 tenants takes major balls. You need to know how to avoid the common pitfalls that can suck up your time and hard-earned money. But, if you do it right, owning your own Section 8 real estate investment property company can pour income from the government straight into your bank account."

Motil, Dr. Matt. *Man on Fire: Lessons from a Perpetual Burnout on Creating Alignment for Success*

First Edition, 2017

"This book was written for anyone that knows their life hasn't reached its full potential, written by someone who has failed repeatedly on the path to alignment and success. Part autobiography, part how-to book, Dr. Matt Motil shares his journey navigating the road of a wanna be real estate investor, perpetual burnout, and closet entrepreneur. Providing lessons learned along the road as an employee, while constantly searching and striving for momentum that ultimately was only achieved after pursuing his passions in real estate."

Nash, R. Nelson. *Becoming Your Own Banker: Unlock the Infinite Banking Concept*

First Edition, 2008

"This book demonstrates that your need for finance, during your lifetime, is much greater than your need for protection."

Taylor, Jeffrey. *The Landlord's Survival Guide: How to Successfully Manage Rental Property as a New or Part-Time Real Estate Investor*

First Edition, 2006

"This concise but comprehensive guide is for first-time—as well as established—landlords. It is divided into sections, each of which is jam-packed with details and insider tips. Most sections will only take minutes to read, and each section tells you exactly what you need to do—and why—to get best results."

Vitale, Joe and Len, Ihaleakala Hew, PhD. *Zero Limits: The Secret Hawaiian System for Wealth, Health, Peace, and More*

First Edition, 2007

"Ho'oponopono is a profound gift that allows one to develop a working relationship with the Divinity within and to learn to ask that in each moment, our errors in thought, word, deed, or action be cleansed. This process is essentially about freedom, complete freedom from the past."

Wicks, Judy. *Good Morning, Beautiful Business: The Unexpected Journey of an Activist Entrepreneur and Local Economy Pioneer*

First Edition, 2013

"Judy Wicks's brilliance redefines what a business can be. The White Dog Café models what commerce will become if we are to create a livable future. This is business as spiritual practice, business as kindness, business as justice, joy, transformation, leadership, and generosity. There is nothing here you will learn in any business school, because the White Dog Café is not in the business of selling life; it's in the business of creating life."

Zelinski, Ernie J. *How to Retire Happy, Wild, and Free: Retirement Wisdom That You Won't Get from Your Financial Advisor*

First Edition, 2004

"This book offers advice on how to enjoy life to its fullest. The key to achieving an active and fulfilling retirement involves a great deal more than having adequate financial resources; it also encompasses all other aspects of life—interesting leisure activities, creative pursuits, physical well-being, mental well-being, and solid social support."

Zuber, Michael. *One Rental at a Time: The Journey to Financial Independence through Real Estate*

First Edition, 2019

"Have you ever thought about real estate investing as a path to financial freedom? Have you kicked around the idea but felt you were too busy with work and family responsibilities? If so, One Rental at a Time *will transform your life, just as it has transformed my life and the lives of others."*

ACKNOWLEDGMENTS

LIKE ANYONE, I am the product of my family, environment, and personal circumstances. One of those circumstances was being diagnosed as dyslexic in the fourth grade. At the time, my mother had me learning to play the piano. When I progressed to playing with both hands, I would freeze up, my mind filled. My parents, both elementary teachers, took me to psychologists for evaluation, and that's how I was diagnosed. In the process, they learned that, in reality, I could barely read at all. I had just been faking it the whole time. Through a long series of programs, I grasped how to learn and read in my own way. By ninth grade I was at the same reading and comprehension level as my other classmates. Kudos to my parents for sticking that out with me and getting me the assistance I needed. It turned out that learning how to learn served me well, and though I was never great in school I did better than I would have otherwise. Failing often and improving a little each day was an early and life-long lesson.

Another influential person in my life was my high school gymnastics coach. He always expected me to do my best and pushed me to surpass even that. In competitive meets, if others were better than me but I had done my best, he was satisfied. If I did not give my best, he knew it and told me so. I was always encouraged but held accountable. He had a rule about no smoking, and because of that I never smoked.

When I contemplated writing this book, it was at a point in my life where I had to overcome the feeling of being a fraud. I am not some huge success story, but Jennifer Bright encouraged me to tell my story. And my story included the interviews of the other investors in this book. The truth of the matter is that there are at least twenty people I know who could have been included in this book. Jennifer's team, some of whom I worked with at Rodale, were instrumental in taking the basic outline I had and transforming it with their design and editorial skills.

And finally, my wife, Sally, of 38+ years deserves a medal for just letting me go about my business of writing this book. She wasn't always aware of what I was doing, but she supported me nonetheless. Her love and encouragement are the soil of my life. It is that simple.

Learning about investing in real estate forced me to hone new skills and take action. Without these lessons, I never would have been confident enough to think I had something worth sharing, let alone writing, and taking action was the key to moving forward. I hope that the lessons shared in this book, as well as the interviews, can teach you something, spur you to take action, and help you step out of your comfort zone so you can live your best life.

ABOUT THE AUTHOR

ROBERT SAYRE, a native of Boulder, moved to the East Coast in 1982 to work at a small book publishing company and then moved to the Lehigh Valley in 1988 to work at Rodale, Inc., as the business manager of its book division, with many great leaders and coworkers. He is now semi-retired, an active investor in real estate, and a volunteer as a master gardener with the Penn State Extension Service, and he has studied and practiced tai chi for 11 years. He and his wife, Sally, a retired public school teacher, have three children and five of the best grandchildren ever. They are as busy as can be, but they love controlling their own schedule and traveling in their Lance RV camper.

www.ingramcontent.com/pod-product-compliance
Lightning Source LLC
Chambersburg PA
CBHW071435210326
41597CB00020B/3810